TALENT SUCCESS: FROM EMPLOYEE RECRUITMENT TO ENGAGEMENT

ANTHONY OPARAUGO

Dedication

To the Chartered Institute of Personnel Management of Nigeria (CIPMN) and the Society for Human Resource Management (SHRM), your unwavering commitment to advancing the HR profession has shaped my journey in profound ways. Your standards, guidance, and communities of practice have enriched my career, strengthened my professional identity, and inspired the insights shared in this book.

About The Author

Anthony Oparaugo, PhD, is a Leadership and Human Resource Management Consultant with extensive experience spanning more than three decades. He built his career in the energy sector, where he rose to the position of Head of Human Resources, overseeing a workforce of more than four thousand employees. In this role, he provided strategic leadership across key HR functions, including recruitment and selection, performance management, training and development, and labor relations. His work in this capacity positioned him as a trusted advisor on organizational effectiveness and workforce strategy. Dr. Oparaugo currently serves as an Assistant Professor of Business Management at the University of Maryland Global Campus in San Diego, where he teaches, mentors, and contributes to the development of future business leaders. His book, ***Talent Success: From Employee Recruitment to Engagement,*** distills his decades of practical and academic expertise into a comprehensive guide for navigating the full spectrum of human resource management. It is an essential resource for HR professionals, business leaders, and students seeking to understand and apply evidence-based talent strategies– ***Gbanju Aruwayo-Obe, PhD.***

Acknowledgements

My deepest gratitude goes to my wife, **Laura**, whose unwavering support has been the quiet strength behind every chapter of this book. Your encouragement, patience, and belief in my work sustained me through long hours of writing and reflection. Thank you for creating the space for me to think, for celebrating every milestone, and for reminding me why this work matters. This book is as much yours as it is mine, and I am profoundly grateful for your love, partnership, and constant inspiration.

Contents

Chapter Four: Employee Onboarding and Socialization 155

Chapter One: Strategic Foundations for Employee Recruitment And Engagement.

Introduction.

Recruitment is not a standalone activity; rather, it is interconnected with several core human resource functions that collectively enhance its effectiveness. It operates as a dynamic and interdependent part of the HR ecosystem that shapes organizational capability, so that it can fulfil its strategic objectives in the area of attracting talent that is aligned with organizational values. This ensures role clarity and supports employee engagement. Recruitment must be informed and reinforced by several HR processes.

In this chapter, we will explore how job analysis, job design, job evaluation, and workforce planning serve as critical antecedents and enablers of strategic recruitment. Each of these functions plays an integral role in reinforcing and optimizing recruitment efforts: job analysis clarifies role expectations and competencies; job design influences motivation and fit; job evaluation ensures internal equity and external competitiveness; and workforce planning aligns recruitment with future organizational needs. By examining these linkages, we will be demonstrating how recruitment is strengthened when embedded within a coherent, evidence-based HR strategy.

JOB ANALYSIS:

Job analysis is one of the most important aspects of human resource management and has formed the hub of all HR activities that are necessary for the successful functioning of organizations. As a human resources activity, it is focused on the collection of work-related information for the job as it currently exists and/or existed in the past or will be in the future. Job analysis is defined as "the process of collecting, analyzing, and setting out information about jobs in order to provide the basis for job description and data for recruitment, training, and job evaluation and performance management" (Armstrong, 2012: 121). It is the process of understanding job details of a specific job and involves the gathering of information through various methods to understand the functions employees perform, the tools and skills employees need, and the results they achieve (Indeed, 2025a & 2025b). Milton (2025) views job analysis as a rigorous process of acquiring information about a job and the human traits required to perform those duties correctly.

From the above definitions, it can be deduced that job analysis is a systematic exploration, study, and recording of the responsibilities, duties, skills, accountabilities, work environment, and abilities required to perform a specific job, and involves determining the relative importance of the duties, responsibilities, and physical and emotional skills for a given job. The systematic investigation is to identify what job demands and what an employee must possess to perform a job productively. The process helps in finding out what a department requires and what a prospective worker needs to perform the job by identifying a job, including job title, job location, job summary, duties involved, working conditions, possible hazards, and machines, tools, equipment, and materials to be used by the existing or potential employees. The process extends to finding out the necessary human qualifications to perform the job. These include establishing the levels of education, experience, judgment, training, initiative, leadership skills, physical skills, communication skills, responsibility, accountability, emotional characteristics, and unusual sensory demands (Rao, 2011; Askarov, 2024). The factors change according to the type, seniority level, industry, and risk involved in a job.

Therefore, job analysis involves the collection of information on the following areas:

- Duties and Tasks: This component focuses on identifying and documenting specific tasks and duties. It involves breaking the job into tasks and understanding how these tasks contribute to the overall organizational mandate. Information to be collected about the tasks may include frequency, duration, effort, skill, complexity, equipment, standards, etc.
- Environment and Conditions: This aspect of job analysis examines the physical and social environment in which

the job is performed. It includes factors such as working hours, physical demands, safety considerations, and any unique conditions or challenges associated with the role. The work environment may include unpleasant conditions such as offensive odor and temperature extremes. There may also be definite risks to the incumbent, such as noxious fumes, radioactive substances, and hostile and aggressive people, and dangerous explosives.

- Tools and Equipment: Some duties and tasks are performed using specific equipment and tools. Equipment may include protective clothing, and other items needed are specified in a job analysis. With the rapid advancement of technology, many jobs now require proficiency in specific tools or software. Job analysis helps identify the technological requirements of a role, ensuring that employees have access to and are trained in the necessary tools to perform their duties effectively.
- Relationships: This component focuses on the interpersonal aspects of the job, including reporting relationships, team dynamics, and interactions with internal and external stakeholders. Understanding these relationships is crucial for fostering effective collaboration and communication within the organization or with external people.
- Requirements: These are the knowledge, skills, and abilities (KSAs) required to perform the job and include technical knowledge, soft skills, and physical abilities necessary for the role. While an incumbent may have higher KSAs than those required for the job, a job analysis typically only states the minimum

requirements to perform the job.

Job Description and Job Specification:

Through systematic investigation of tasks, duties, and responsibilities necessary to do a specific job, job analysis produces two major documents that are required for recruitment purposes, namely, job description and job specification. A job description is a well-written duty statement that contains action words that accurately describe what is to be done, defining accountability in the organization, and helping to summarize duties. As an action-based document, it focuses on primary, current, normal, and daily duties and responsibilities of a job position. For example, it clarifies work functions and reporting relationships, helping employees understand their jobs and outlining the essential duties and responsibilities that are expected of them and the basic purpose of the work that the employee is expected to perform. Below is a sample of a job description.

Figure 1.1: Sample (template) of Job Description.

JOB TITLE	AGM (HR & Admin. Services)		
Company	ABC Ltd	Location San Diego	ABC Ltd
Job Grade	SMI	Interfaces: CEO, AGM (F&A), AGM (CS), AGM (Legal)	
Minimum educational specification BSc. (Human Resources) or its equivalent		Professional membership: MCIPM, MCIPD, etc.	

JOB OBJECTIVES(S)
Planning and implementation of Human Resource activities in the company; implementation of efficient administration and services

REPORTING RELATIONSHIPS
Functionally reports to: CEO
Administratively reports to: CEO
SUPERVISES: Principal Manager (HR) and Principal Manager (Admin. & Services)

DUTIES & RESPONSIBILITIES

<ul><li>Human Resources Strategy implementation</li><li>Recruitment, selection and placement</li><li>Reward management</li><li>Performance management</li><li>Learning and development</li><li>Employee discipline and grievance management</li><li>Succession planning</li></ul>	<ul><li>Occupational health and safety</li><li>Employee engagement</li><li>Others</li></ul>

KEY PERFORMANCE INDICATORS

<ul><li>Motivated staff</li><li>Number of staff attrition rate</li><li>Low rate of accident</li><li>Improvement labor relations</li></ul>	<ul><li>Cultural change</li><li>Internal customer satisfaction</li><li>Teamwork</li><li>Staff productivity level</li></ul>

KEY COMPETENCY REQUIREMENTS

<ul><li>IT skills</li><li>Report writing skills</li><li>Human relation skills</li><li>Motivation skill</li></ul>	<ul><li>Communication skills</li><li>Conflict management skills</li><li>Training skill</li><li>Bargaining skills</li></ul>

A job description must reflect the positions/work as contained in the organization's structure. The organization structure outlines both formal reporting lines and informal relationships among individuals and positions. In large organizations, the prevailing model is often bureaucratic, characterized by multiple hierarchical levels, a top-down management approach, and rigid boundaries between roles and departments. As a result, job descriptions in such settings tend to be narrowly defined, emphasizing specialization and limited cross- functional interaction.

Conversely, flat organizations operate with fewer management layers and embrace a decentralized approach. In these environments, job roles are broadly defined, and job descriptions are designed to be flexible. The boundaries between roles and units are more permeable, fostering collaboration, teamwork, and cross-functional engagement. Teams serve as the foundational units of flat and boundary-less organizations, sharing expertise and holding mutual accountability for outcomes.

Developing a job description begins with a thorough job analysis, which includes job specification, job evaluation, job design, and workflow analysis. Workflow analysis, in particular, examines how work is structured to align with the organization's strategic objectives. It traces the journey of a product or service from customer demand through internal processes, highlighting how employee competencies add value at each stage. This analysis may also reveal opportunities to merge, simplify, or eliminate certain roles to enhance efficiency and alignment with organizational goals. As competition and technological innovations increase, jobs are becoming less individually based, and the tasks to perform are becoming more volatile and more team-based (Edien, 2015).

Job Specification.

A job specification is a detailed statement highlighting qualifications, skills, experience, and personal attributes required for a person to successfully perform a specific job, and provides the basis for recruiting qualified job candidates, while at the same time discouraging unqualified applicants. It recognizes the skills that are relevant to specific tasks, which may include: education; experience; specialized training; personal attributes or abilities; and the physical demands of the job (Mangaleswaran and Kirushanthan, 2015). The difference between a job description and a job specification is that the former focuses on the duties and responsibilities, while the latter zeroes in on the person who is to do the job. As a logical outgrowth of a job description, a job specification helps organizations determine the type of employees who will take up specific Jobs. The content of the job specification is given below:

Strategic Importance of Job Analysis.

Job analysis is an essential human resource tool and the starting point of human resource activities. It reveals the overall purpose of a job, why it exists, and what the job holder is expected to contribute; the qualifications of the employee that make them suitable for this position; who the job holder reports to, and those that report to the job holder; and the scope of the job to be carried out. The importance of job analysis cannot be overemphasized: it is the strategic lever that connects people, processes, performance, and aligns talent with organizational goals (Keeler et al, 2022; Coursera, 2024; Wonders et al, 2025). Below are some ways job analysis can play strategic roles:

- Alignment with organizational strategy: Job analysis prescribes how organizational resources could be used to ensure that every role within the organization contributes meaningfully to strategic objectives. This is done by clarifying the task involved and the knowledge, skills, and abilities required to carry it out. Whether the priority is enhancing customer experience, innovation, ensuring regulatory compliance, or driving growth, HR professionals can leverage job analysis to optimize the deployment of talents and, at the same time, maintain agility and flexibility in response to shifting business demands. It is a powerful tool for collecting information and designing interventions that fuel sustainable success.
- Employee recruitment and selection: Recruitment and selection processes largely leverage information from job analysis, such as job descriptions and specifications, to write accurate job postings, which are essential for attracting and selecting the right candidates. A well-conducted job analysis provides a realistic view of what

employees in a particular role do and offers concise insight into a particular position's essential knowledge and capabilities. This information helps recruiters identify the qualifications, experience, and behavioral traits needed for success in a role and forms part of the job-related selection criteria, as well as interview questions. An understanding of the vacancies and the skills needed will help an organization in its recruitment strategy. In other words, it ensures that organizations recruit candidates who align best with their business needs.

- Performance management: Role clarity and expectations derived from job analysis allow for fair and objective performance reviews. The issue of efficient performance is very important to any organization. Job analysis helps to identify the tasks to be performed and the standard of performance expected. By comparing what is expected to be done and what has been done, an organization will be able to determine whether it is on track or not. By extension, it ascertains whether employees possess the necessary competence to fulfill their roles and where there are gaps, trainings are used to properly equip the employees to the level of proficiency required.

- Supporting compliance and equity: Job analysis establishes the foundation for determining whether or not employment practices and choices are carried out in compliance with the relevant laws. It helps ensure that organizations are in compliance with labor laws, equal employment opportunity regulations, and occupational health standards. For example, organizational jobs have to be properly analyzed to accommodate women, disabled persons, minorities, etc., to avoid violation of certain labor laws. In the case of petitions, it provides defensible documents to support hiring, promotion, compensation, and termination, thereby reducing bias and vulnerability to litigation.

- Promoting employee engagement: Job analysis enhances employee engagement when employees understand their roles, responsibilities, and how their work contributes to the organization's big picture. Job analysis can be used to identify factors that shape employees'
- Motivation and job satisfaction, and engagement, through accurate information on jobs and responsibilities, as well as the level of performance required. This provides employees with clear direction on how to go about with a view to achieving desired results. For example, a job description and performance standard that is regularly updated gives the workers a better understanding of the company's expectations relating to production and service delivery standards. Role clarity, in turn, improves employees' morale, job satisfaction, and productivity, and helps HR professionals to eliminate unnecessary job requirements, areas of conflict, and dissatisfaction. In addition, onboarding and socialization efforts are strengthened when job analysis provides a transparent roadmap of responsibilities and performance metrics, thus helping new employees integrate more effectively into the organizational culture and processes.
- Facilitating organizational design and change management: In the process of job analysis, we can learn what people do in their roles, and this realistic

perspective uncovers the true nature of work, enabling management to identify areas that need improvement or make informed decisions about job design and resource allocation. More so, in times of organizational reengineering, mergers, and acquisitions, job analysis becomes vital for redesigning workflows and roles. The strategic implication is that some jobs can be merged, simplified, or eliminated. Also, new jobs can be designed to support emerging business needs, and this flexibility is necessary for maintaining a competitive edge in a dynamic marketplace. In a situation where employees usually perform tasks that differ from their original job description, this creates insights into the actual things workers are doing and provides an opportunity for them to reflect on their own methods of working, adjusting the time spent on certain tasks, which can lead to innovative ideas or changes in behavior. This self-reflective process can foster new ideas, ownership, and lead to behavioral shifts that support innovation and continuous improvement.

In addition to the above-mentioned uses, the cost data captured in job analysis can be used to develop an organization's overall budget. This will give the managers or workers further insight as to how to plan each work schedule and cost centers with a view to meeting the estimated figures. It can also measure whether the estimates were met at the end of the accounting period; by so doing, it helps the organization's leaders to monitor the overall performance of the organization. Job analysis aids business concerns to identify cost-saving opportunities, thereby controlling expenditure.

Job analysis plays a very important role in carrying out effective decision-making, which improves services and employee performance. It does this by showing the cost and benefit of each project, helping in the planning and prudent management of resources in the organization. According to Edien (2015), job analysis as a tool for business decision-making provides the following advantages:

- It requires all levels of management to plan and formalize goals on a repetitive basis.
- It provides definite objectives for evaluating performance at each level of responsibility.
- It creates an early warning system for potential problems so that management can make changes before they get out of hand.
- It facilitates the coordination of activities within the organization by segment and divisional goals to align with the company's mandate.
- The results in greater management awareness of the company's overall operations, including the impact of external factors such as economic trends.
- Motivates the workforce throughout the organization to meet planned objectives.

Proactively, the analysis serves as an invaluable source of feedback to develop some useful programs like job rotation, job enlargement, and job enrichment to achieve a better match between job demands and employee competencies. Generally, the experience of most companies indicates a positive impact on job analysis leading to greater administrative efficiency, cost savings, better organizational climate, and improved productivity in the form of sales and profit, and provides a foundation for all human resource planning activities. This is because organizations facing environmental turbulence will call on HR experts to develop approaches that will capture changes in the job and work environment, constantly updating their human resource information systems (HRIS) and placing employees in jobs for which they possess special competencies. Consequently, companies will be able to refine their competitive strategies to make optimal use of the unique strengths of their workforce (Siddique, 2004; Edien, 2015).

However, the analysis of a job does not guarantee that the managers or organization will get the desired output. Collecting and recording information for a specific job involves several complications. If the job information is not accurate and not checked from time to time, an employee will not be able to perform their duty well. Until and unless he is not aware of what he is supposed to do or what is expected of him, chances are that the time and energy spent on a particular job analysis is a sheer wastage of human resources. Therefore, proper care should be taken while conducting a job analysis. A thorough and unbiased investigation or study of a specific job is good for both the managers and the employees. The managers get to know who to hire and why. They can fill a place with the right person. On the other hand, an existing or potential employee gets to know what and how he is supposed to perform the job and what the desired output is. Job analysis creates the right fit between the job and the employee.

Sources of Collecting Job Analysis Data:

There are many ways of collecting job analysis data. Some of them are discussed below:

Personal Observation:

When workers perform their jobs, the job analyst, i.e., the subject matter expert, observes and receives firsthand information to assess some job factors such as social demand, physical hazards, and emotional and mental pressures. A job analyst observes an employee and records all his performed and non-performed tasks, fulfilled and unfulfilled responsibilities and duties, methods, ways, and skills used by him or her to perform various duties. Here, the subject matter expert observes the workers while on the job, taking notice of the task involved, and the pace at which it is carried out, the working conditions, and the behavior required for doing the job. This is the simplest and least expensive source or method of collecting information. However, it is not problem-free, as employees tend to perform better when they are watched, and this makes it difficult to observe "normal" work performance. This phenomenon is known in the management circle as the "Hawthorne Effect"- a name derived from a study conducted at Westinghouse Hawthorne Relay Assembly

Works Plant in Chicago. It was observed that productivity improved when the lighting level increased, and surprisingly, when the light was dimmed, productivity also improved. It was therefore concluded that improvement in productivity was related to the fact that someone was paying attention to the employees. Another problem could be biased towards specific employees; difficulty may occur in selecting representative employees to observe (whether it is the best, worst, or average). It is particularly useful for jobs that involve tangible, observable tasks, but may not be easy to observe work that is intellectually oriented, in which much time is spent thinking and planning. Hence, it may not be suitable (as the only method) in analyzing the top managers' jobs who spend lots of time thinking and solving organizational challenges that may not be easily observed. That is to say that it may not be suitable for roles that involve significant cognitive work or decision-making processes that are not readily visible.

Job Performance Method:

While the job analyst can observe job holders perform their jobs, he can shadow the employees by performing their roles to understand the job better. In the process, the job analyst may answer emails, perform physical tasks, and interact with colleagues or systems to learn what an employee experiences. Having gathered first-hand experience, he can determine what some of the issues and requirements are and how companies might properly detail these in a job description.

Instead of solely observing employees as they perform their duties, a job analyst may immerse themselves in the role by shadowing and actively participating in the tasks. This experiential approach allows the analyst to engage in activities such as responding to emails, completing physical tasks, and interacting with colleagues or systems, gaining a deeper understanding of the employee's day-to-day experience. Through this firsthand involvement, the analyst can identify key challenges, responsibilities, and requirements, enabling organizations to craft more accurate and meaningful job descriptions.

Critical Incidents:

This technique is used for task identification. It involves having the individuals who are familiar with the job record incidents of particularly effective and ineffective behavior that they have seen on the job over a period of time. With this method, the job holders are asked to describe several incidents based on their past experience, for example, a worker in an animal farm outfit whose primary duty is to extract milk from cows, the critical incidents involved may include: prepare 200 cows; examine cows for health problems, clean milking equipment, and milking room after milking; perform preventive maintenance on the milking equipment, etc. The critical incidents are recorded after the events have taken place. The incidents collected are analyzed and classified according to the job areas they describe. The advantage is that the method is an excellent way to develop learning materials that show employees how work should be performed. The disadvantage is that it takes a considerable length of time to compile to give a complete picture of the job.

Interviews:

In this method, employees are interviewed directly by a job analyst so that they come up with their own working styles, problems faced by them, use of particular skills and techniques while performing their jobs, and insecurities and fears about their careers. The analysts can gather information about the employee's responsibilities, tools, and unique work approaches through discussions. With this method, questions are asked to both the incumbent and the supervisors either in a group or personally. The data from interviews can be used as a supplement in the process of job analysis. Also, knowledgeable senior job incumbents could be requested to outline the critical aspects of the jobs that need to be taken into consideration. The interaction with these senior members of staff can help extract information for job analysis. The challenge in getting job analysis information from job holders is that, oftentimes, some of them naturally tend to overstate the importance and the requirements of their job. This may result in what is known as the "Heisenberg Effect," a situation where employees give answers that they think the interviewer wants to hear. To reduce this incidence, information can be collected from several workers, and to get the true job-related information, organizations should effectively communicate to the staff that the data collected will be used for their own good. It is very important to ensure that it will not be used against them in any way. If it is not done properly, it will be a sheer wastage of time, money, and human resources.

Job Diaries and Inventory Methods:

With this method, job incumbents are advised to keep diaries of their activities, the time spent, the task involved, the different aspects, physical and mental requirements, etc. This can be an objective way to understand how employees spend their time and can identify areas where an employee might shift their attention to more important responsibilities. These will form the data that the job analyst will adopt in his job analysis. On the other hand, job inventory involves a structured checklist that employees can check off to confirm that they have completed a certain task. The aim is to ensure that they have met a comprehensive list of tasks associated with a job in terms of expectations; requisite qualifications, using the right tools; and the frequency, importance, and difficulty involved in task completion.

Questionnaires:

These are predefined questions designed to solicit job-related information such as employees' perspectives on their environment, resources, support, and the demands of the job. This method is cost-effective and may include asking employees about how they spend each day, what their priorities are, and how they effectively perform their duties.

Deciding how often to carry out job analysis would depend on how the organization needs it. Some companies would like to review it annually; others may choose to review job positions after several years. It is advisable to use supervisors and job incumbents to obtain information about jobs in an organization. External analysts who know about the job can also be used to cross-check the analysis done by in- house staff. The jobs to be analyzed are those that are critical for the success of the organization or those that are difficult to learn or perform. The other conditions in which job analysis can take place include the introduction of new technology, when completely different jobs are added, and when some jobs are subsumed into other jobs within the organization. Job analysis, when properly conducted, gives insight into the job description, job specification, job evaluation, and job design/structure. By identifying skill gaps, organizations use them to ensure that employees have the skills and competencies needed to perform their roles effectively and to foster employee engagement.

Having discussed the strategic role of job analysis, it is not without its challenges. Some of the obstacles that organizations face include the following:

- Rapidly changing job roles: Everything around us is changing fast due to technological advancement, particularly in information and communication technology, and what it requires of organizations to adopt agile and flexible processes to regularly review and update job information.

- Subjectivity and bias: Sometimes, subjectivity may creep into the job analysis process, and overcoming bias requires using multiple methods and sources of information to validate the findings.
- Time-consuming: It is time-consuming and resource-intensive, especially for large organizations with multiple job roles.
- Employees' resistance: Employees and their unions may not want to participate in job analysis, particularly when they fear it might lead to exit or reduced remuneration; hence, effective communication may be required to allow for employee buy-in.
- Intangible aspect of some jobs: Some jobs may have certain aspects that are difficult to measure or capture quantitatively; HR experts should look for alternative ways of capturing them qualitatively and not ignore them.

Job Design:

Job design refers to the process used by organizations to create meaningful roles and responsibilities for employees so as to maximize both employee job satisfaction and performance, and ensure all employees are set up for success (Bhasin, 2025). It is the process that companies use to create new jobs or add to an existing job to enable them to achieve their goals by having more employees perform more within the organization (Indeed, 20205c). According to Torrington et al (2011), this is the technique of putting together a range of tasks, duties, and responsibilities to create a composite for employees to undertake in their work and own it, not only as the basis of individual satisfaction and achievement, but necessity in getting the job done efficiently, economically, reliably, and safely.

As an offshoot of job analysis, it is concerned with modifying, changing, and enriching jobs in order to capture job candidates or improve the engagement of existing employees while improving organizational performance. It is a logical arrangement of a job that involves specifying the content of the job, the work methods used in its performance, and how the job relates to other jobs in the organization. Job design can be initiated or led by the managers (top-down) or by the workers (bottom-up) (Daniel et al, 2017). In designing jobs, at least four elements need to be considered, namely, job content, job context, work relationship, and line manager (Engage for Success, 2014). The job content contains information about various job activities included in a specific job. It is a detailed account of actions that an employee needs to perform during their tenure. The actual content of the job should be designed to enable people to find their work meaningful. In addition, people need to have a sense of responsibility and be able to see the link between the works they do and the end results of their work. Where possible, job content needs to allow people to use their current skills and develop new ones; see how their work contributes to the big picture; feel that the work they do matters and makes a difference; have a sense of autonomy, and receive regular and constructive feedback. The following information about the content of the job is necessary for good job design:

- Duties of an employee
- What an employee does
- Machines, tools, and equipment are to be used while performing a specific job.
- Additional tasks involved in a job
- Desired output level (What is expected of an employee?)
- Type of training, competencies, personal characteristics, and educational qualifications required

Secondly, the job context refers to the situation or condition under which an employee performs a job. This includes factors such as ergonomic job design, work setting, technology, and flexible working options. When designing jobs, these contextual features all need to be taken into consideration; we know that a sense of autonomy arises in part when employees feel they have some choice and control over the context within which they work. Equally, to experience the 'safety' that Kahn (1990) notes to be so vital for engagement, employees need to feel their job is environmentally and ergonomically healthy. The needful information can be summed up as:

- Working Conditions
- Risks involved
- Whom to report to
- Who will all employees report to?
- Hazards

- Physical and mental demands
- Judgment, etc.

The third aspect is the work relationship, and common sense tells us that people are more likely to be engaged in organizations with harmonious work settings, trust, and open communication. Moreso, jobs in the modern economy are more likely to be inter-dependent, and so job design needs to consider not just the job itself, but also the way the job holders interact with those around them.

The fourth factor is the role of the line managers, which is vital in bringing job design and its implementation into reality. Simply having a well-designed job will count for nothing with an unsupportive line manager who provides no feedback. Line managers can help to create an environment where workers can find their work engaging, through shaping job content, the kind of treatment or trust reposed in the employees, and designing meaningful work jobs in which employees will feel physically and psychologically safe in performing their work.

Taken together, these four elements will need to be considered when determining how to design jobs optimally. The best solution will vary depending on job content and the job context. A job can be designed in such a way as to match the employees' resources (competencies) if they are to be engaged. These resources can be personal resources that the individual brings with them to work, such as their skills and abilities, including tangible and physical resources, such as equipment, and positive and empowering leadership. However, designing jobs that promote employee recruitment and engagement would require consideration of some other factors, such as the organizational, environmental, and behavioral components of the workplace. Details of this can be found in the last chapter of this book.

Strategic Importance of Job Design:

Job design is a strategic element of human resource practice that shapes how jobs are structured, executed, and experienced within an organization. It is an intentional organization of tasks, responsibilities, and workflows to enhance both organizational efficiency and employee well-being (Anderson and Caldwell, 2018; David, 2025. With the fast- paced and competitive nature of business today, the importance of effective job design in improving employee productivity cannot be overemphasized. Job design is very important for the organization due to its benefits as follows:

Support organizational strategy:

Job design is no longer a mere administrative function, but a strategic imperative in aligning individual roles with organizational goals, shaping employee experiences, and driving sustainable competitive advantage. Its strategic importance emanates from the intentional restructuring of roles, tasks, and workflows to support the organization's long-term objectives. As companies grapple with the digital economy and transformations, there has been a need to design and redesign jobs with flexibility and agility to address talent shortages, shifting workforce expectations, and, at the same time, priorities like innovation, customer centricity, operational efficiency, and employee engagement. This is a paradigm shift from traditional task allocation to how jobs contribute to value creation, adaptability, and strategic differentiation. It aims at aligning individual roles to strategic goals, enhancing agility and innovation. Strategic job design accelerates the optimal deployment of skills and capabilities, and this is by aligning roles with employee strengths and developmental pathways to maximize productivity and support the succession pipeline. Also, employer branding and employee retention can be strengthened through jobs that offer meaning, growth, and alignment with personal values, which contribute to a compelling employee value proposition, which in turn enhances employee recruitment, retention, and engagement. In order to achieve strategic alignment, organizations are crafting jobs that encourage employees to tailor their roles within strategic boundaries, accommodate remote work while maintaining strategic coherence, and assign tasks around strategic competencies. The modern job designs have become a strategic tool that helps organizations execute their vision, engage their people, and adapt to change.

Recruitment and selection:

Job design specifies the job content and context, as well

as the procedures for performing the task and other information required in designing organizational structure. Organizational structure is defined as the formal system of how tasks, responsibilities, authority, and communication are arranged within an organization. This serves as the framework that guides how work flows, decisions are made, and goals are achieved. It helps the organization know what exists (job description) and information on the skills, knowledge, and abilities required (job specification), which provides a milestone to select competent new employees who are capable of performing the task well in the organization. In other words, job design is pivotal in shaping recruitment and selection processes by influencing how advertised roles are perceived by job candidates and ultimately filled. It can impact recruitment and selection in these ways:

- Offers attraction to job candidates: A thoughtfully designed job offers task variety, autonomy, role clarity, and growth opportunities that appeal to prospective employees.
- Streamlines selection process: It helps recruiters identify the right skills and abilities during interviews, improving the quality of hire and reducing the tendency of mismatches.
- Clarity in job description: Job design provides clear job descriptions and specifications. These two documents are used to help job candidates understand expectations, responsibilities, and qualifications required.

Motivation and commitment of employees:

A good job description helps employees to put in their efforts for the success of the company. This is achieved by engaging in meaningful work that creates a sense of accomplishment, purpose, and pride, thereby boosting job satisfaction and morale, and creating a positive work environment. Properly designed jobs have a way of assigning roles and responsibilities to increase motivation and reduce job duty confusion and burnout. Some aspects of the job design involving autonomy, skill variety, task significance, feedback mechanism, and growth opportunities stimulate intrinsic motivation, allowing employees to work at their optimal potential and surpass expectations (Hackman & Oldham, 1975; Daniel et al, 2017). One of the aims of job design is to make the work more interesting and challenging. It is not only that interesting and challenging jobs provide better pay for employees, it inspire them to greater job performance. In addition to motivation, it brings a high degree of commitment in employees towards organizational goals and objectives.

Improves employees' physical and mental health:

In today's world of work, the correlation between job design and employee health and its impact on organizational success cannot be ignored. More importantly, the connection has gone beyond the traditional practice of health and safety into the more delicate realm of mental well–being. A well–designed job solves problems relating to overloading or under loading of work; isolation, repetitive, and shift work-related issues and problems connected with excessive working hours. This is with the view of reducing the risk of physical and mental health issues. Tasks are usually varied to prevent physical ailments such as musculoskeletal disorders and injuries. It is also designed to determine the extent of muscular energy required for a particular task in such a way as to minimize energy expenditure. Job designs that offer task autonomy, task significance, and opportunities for skill development promote a sense of purpose and achievement, which are all essential for mental health. On the other hand, monotonous or overly demanding roles can lead to stress, burnout, and other mental health issues. Breaks, time-offs, and flexible work hours are integrated into job designs to combat physical and mental fatigue, and, similarly, jobs are designed to match skills, interests, and workload capacity of the employee to reduce stress, avoid burnout, and improve well-being.

Employee engagement:

One of the major drivers of employee engagement is job design, though often overlooked, it encompasses the way roles, tasks, and responsibilities are structured within an organization. Thoughtful job designs not only enhance organizational performance but also foster a sense of purpose, autonomy, feedback mechanisms, skill utilization, and role clarity, which together drive employee engagement. The elements of job design that drive employee engagement by creating roles that are meaningful, manageable, and motivating are highlighted below:

- Task variety incorporates diverse job activities that keep employees mentally and physically stimulated, thereby reducing monotonous work that leads to disengagement and burnout.
- The autonomy integrated into job designs gives employees control, ownership, and accountability of their tasks, and leads to intrinsic motivation and employee engagement.
- Feedback mechanisms that are regular and constructive help in performance management and reinforce values within the organization. It drives employee engagement and creates a sense of pride when people become aware of how their efforts are contributing to the success of the organization.
- Role clarity reduces ambiguity and stress and leads to engagement when employees understand their responsibilities.
- Creating jobs that allow employees to utilize and develop their competencies signals that the organizations are invested in its people and leads to engagement.

In a nutshell, job design creates work and a work environment that are meaningful, challenging, and supportive so that employees will feel empowered, valued, and aligned with the organization's mission. It is a strategic tool that unlocks the full potential of the workforce and accelerates engagement and organizational performance, and consequently leads to higher levels of discretionary efforts on the part of the employees; reduced turnover rate; improved mental well-being and collaboration.

Organizational Productivity:

Productivity is tied to several organizational variables that have a connection with job design, such as operational efficiency, employee motivation, skill utilization, reduced turnover and absenteeism, among others. A good job design streamlines workflow, eliminates redundancies, and minimizes wasted effort, resulting in enhanced operational efficiency and resource optimization. For instance, clearly defined roles reduce redundancies and confusion, and allow employees to focus on high-impact tasks, while streamlined workflows minimize delays and bottlenecks, enhancing operational efficiency. Also, jobs are designed to match employees' strengths and competencies, and this alignment reduces errors, increases quality, and accelerates task completion. At a time when agility and efficiency are needed, investing in smart job design is not just beneficial but essential. It is leveraging some strategies to improve productivity, and some of them are as follows:

- Creating jobs that offer autonomy, purpose, and opportunities for growth fosters intrinsic motivation.
- Providing engaging and meaningful work to reduce burnout and dissatisfaction.
- Incorporating feedback mechanisms into job designs to

improve performance management systems

- Using job rotation and enrichment to stimulate employees to higher productivity
- Leveraging technology to handle monotonous tasks, thereby freeing up time for strategic work.
- Using diverse perspectives and cross-functional work designs to encourage innovation, teamwork, and transfer of knowledge.

Environmental adaptation:

By environmental adaptation, we refer to the ability of individuals and organizations to adjust to external changes. The changes may be physical, such as workplace layout and machines, or the social dynamics, like remote work and team structures, and ecological factors like sustainable goals. Given the rapid technological change, climate challenges, and evolving workplace norms, companies are trying to maintain the flow by restructuring jobs to align with the social, physical, and technological work environment and how people perform, collaborate, and bring about innovations. Practical strategies being inculcated in job designs to achieve environmental adaptation include:

- Integrating ergonomic principles, flexible workspaces, remote work options, and moderating tasks and schedules based on environmental conditions like heat, noise, and lighting.
- Promoting sustainability through eco-conscious practices like waste reduction, optimizing energy use,

sourcing materials sustainably, and aligning employees with organizational values, thereby contributing to environmental goals.

- Job design that includes autonomy and task variety empowers employees to respond swiftly to environmental changes, such as supply chain disruptions or climate-related challenges.
- It fosters collaboration, diversity, and inclusion, which equips employees to adapt in a shifting social environment.

Labor relations:

Labor relations imply the interaction between workers and their representative (labor unions), the employer represented by management, and the government and its agencies.

When an organization thoughtfully designs its jobs to align with employee expectations and organizational values, it fosters trust, collaboration, and mutual respect and creates a foundation for positive labor-management relations. Conversely, if jobs are not properly structured, it may lead to low morale, industrial disputes, strikes, and lockouts. What it means is that job design plays a vital role in the shaping of labor relations, especially in those areas where labor unions represent their members, such as working conditions, rights, and responsibilities of the employees. By crafting roles that are fair, engaging, and responsive to employee needs, organizations can promote a culture of collaboration and mutual respect and minimize areas of conflict. These strategies can be integrated into job design to minimize labor-management disputes:

- Jobs that incorporate clarity, purpose, and growth can reduce dissatisfaction, industrial disputes, and the tendency of employees to seek the intervention of their unions.
- Job clarity and a feedback mechanism foster transparency and open communication, which strengthens labor relations and reduces misunderstanding and conflict.
- When jobs are designed to be specific, measurable, attainable, relevant, and time-bound (SMART), it makes negotiations between labor and management more straightforward and equitable.
- Integrating ergonomic principles and psychological safety into job designs to reduce workplace stress and injuries may be a demonstration of management commitment to improving labor relations.

Job Evaluation:

Job evaluation is a systematic way of determining the value/worth of a job in relation to other jobs in an organization (Rao, 2011). It tries to use formal and systematic procedures to determine the relative worth of a job for the purpose of establishing a rational pay structure. Susanto et al (2024) define it as the process of determining the relative value or the contribution of each position or job in an organization in order to establish an acceptable salary structure. What it entails is that each job would undergo a thorough examination using well-defined criteria such as responsibility, task complexity, competencies required to carry out the job, and the job's impact on the strategic goal of the company. Other criteria include physical efforts, working conditions, experience, the extent to which the worker can work without supervision, etc. These factors are used to rate jobs in a business entity by establishing their value in a job hierarchy and then comparing them with other jobs to determine their value contributions. The value a job/worker produces reflects the pay attached to such a job. While often associated with compensation and internal equity, job evaluation plays a critical role in shaping recruitment strategies, employee engagement, job descriptions, workforce planning, succession planning, and performance management. In other words, the goal is to support the strategic initiatives of organizations in terms of a fair and consistent framework for compensation, career progression, and organizational structure.

Though job evaluation provides a basis for developing a differential wage structure, it must be remembered that it is about estimates and not absolutes. That is to say that it cannot be the sole factor for determining what a worker receives as his/her wages. There are some external factors that play a vital role in determining pay packages, such as the labor market conditions, collective bargaining, government interventions in the form of legislation, inflation rate, etc.

It is pertinent to mention that the starting point for job evaluation is Job Analysis. No job can be accurately evaluated until it is analyzed. Every job evaluation method requires at least some basic job analysis to provide some information concerning that job. Therefore, job evaluation begins with job analysis and ends at the point where the worth of the job is determined.

For a job evaluation system to be effective, care must be taken to ensure the system is as objective as possible. It is important that each job is evaluated based on current, regular, and ongoing work conditions and job content. It is also essential that the focus of the evaluation process be on the purpose, scope, and responsibilities of work assigned to the position, and not an incumbent's personal qualities or performance. In other words, the focus is on the position and not the individual(s) in the position.

As jobs are very often affected in some way by organizational change, maintaining the job evaluations system requires that departments periodically review their organization design and structure to determine if significant changes have occurred. Any change in an organization's structure may alter the content of a job, which may result in an adjustment in the evaluation of the job. Ideally, the position description should be updated every time there is a substantial change to a position's purpose, scope, and/or responsibilities.

Methods of Job Evaluation:

Generally, there are two types of job evaluation methods, i.e., non- qualitative methods and qualitative methods. The basic difference between the two methods lies in the fact that, under non-qualitative methods, a job is compared as a whole with other jobs in the organization, whereas in the case of qualitative methods, the key factors are selected and then measured. The job evaluation methods are discussed in detail below, and the most common ones are ranking, grading, factor comparison, and point methods (Cascio, 2018; SHRM, 2019).

Ranking or Job Comparison Method:

This is one of the non- qualitative techniques in job evaluation. It simply lists the relative worth of the various jobs examined. Jobs are arranged from the highest to the lowest, in order of their value or merit to the organization. The importance of jobs is judged in terms of duties, responsibilities, and demands on the job holder. The jobs are examined and ranked as a whole rather than based on important factors in the job. It is most suitable in small organizations where many jobs are not involved. This is a simple method of evaluation that is best suited for small organizations. It is economical to use and less. It is not suitable for large organizations because rankings are difficult and complex when the number of jobs is large. There is no definite standard of judgment, and there is no way of measuring the differences between jobs, coupled with their subjective nature, which may offend many employees. The example of the ranking method is demonstrated below:

Table 1.1: Example of Ranking Method

S/NO	RANKING ORDER	MONTHLY SALARIES
1.	Chief Executive Officer	$20, 000
2.	Assistant General Managers	$15,000
3.	Principal Managers	$12,000
4.	Senior Managers	$10,000
5.	Managers	$8,000
6.	Officers	$5,000
7.	Clerical Assistants	$3,000

The jobs are first ranked in each unit and department and then combined to develop an organizational ranking. The variation in payment of salaries depends on the nature of the job performed by the employees. The following processes may be involved (Khanka, 2007):

- Analyze and describe jobs, bringing out those aspects that are to be used for job ranking.
- Identify benchmark jobs (List of jobs which include all the major departments and functions).
- Rank all jobs in the organization around the benchmark jobs until all jobs are placed in the rank order of

importance.

- Finally, divide all the ranked jobs into appropriate groups by considering the common features of the jobs (i.e., those that are similar in their duties and performance, require similar skills and training, etc.). All the jobs within a group or ranking receive the same wage or a range of wages.

The underlying principle is that grades or classes are established, and then jobs are selected and placed into appropriate grades depending on how the characteristics fit in a grade and the salaries attached to it. This method is simple and easy to understand, it takes into account all the factors that make the job, and can be used for a variety of jobs and organizations. The grouping of jobs into classifications not only makes pay determination easy but also makes it acceptable to almost all workers. Though it is difficult to write an all-inclusive description of a grade, when a job does not fit into a grade, and there is no other grade for it, it is lumped into any available grade. It suffers from the personal bias of those carrying out the job evaluation and may oversimplify sharp differences between different jobs and different grades.

Factor Comparison Method:

This is a qualitative Method. The method combines both ranking and point methods. It evaluates jobs by comparing them and makes further analysis by breaking them into compensable factors. Instead of ranking complete jobs, each job is ranked according to a series of factors, such as mental effort. Physical effort, the skill needed, responsibility, supervision level, working conditions, etc. This is further illustrated below:

Table 1.2: Example of factor comparison method of evaluation.

		Compensable Factors					
S/N O	Job Title	Physical Effort	Mental effort	Skill	Responsibility	Working Conditions	Wage Rate Per Day
1.	Secretary	$30	$70	$70	$60	$30	$260
2.	Driver	$70	$40	$50	$40	$30	$230
3.	Receptionist	$30	$50	$50	$50	$40	$220
4.	Typist	$30	$40	$50	$50	$30	$210
5.	Clerk	$40	$50	$40	$50	$40	$200

This is a more analytical and objective job evaluation method. The method provides flexibility as there is no upper limitation on the rating of a factor. When compared with all other jobs in terms of key factors, it is relatively valid and attaches money values in a fair way based on an agreed rank order fixed by the job evaluation committee. However, it is more time-consuming and expensive, with some difficulties in understanding, explaining, and operating. Its use of the same five criteria to assess all the jobs is questionable because jobs differ across and within organizations.

Point Method of Job Evaluation:

Under this method, jobs are broken down based on various identifiable factors such as experience, skill, physical effort, mental effort, responsibility, risk-taking initiatives, etc. Points are attached to each of these factors after prioritizing them in order of their importance. The procedures involved in determining job points are as follows:

- First, determine the jobs to be evaluated: The jobs must cover all the major occupational functions.
- Identify the factors common: Identify the factors common to all the identified jobs, such as skill, responsibility, etc.
- Define the factors clearly in writing: This is necessary to ensure that different job raters interpret a factor in the same sense. For example, the key factors can be defined thus: Skill: This includes education, training, experience, social skills, problem-solving skills, degree of direction, creative thinking, use of judgment, etc. Responsibility/Accountability: This included the breadth of responsibility, specialized responsibility, complexity of work, degree of freedom to act, the nature and number of subordinate employees, the extent of accountability for products and materials, etc. Effort: Mental demands of a job, physical demands of a job, degree of potential stress.
- Determine the maximum number of points: Determine the maximum number of points to assign to each factor, and sum up the point values for each job to establish the worth.

- Convert total points to monetary values: Hence, the worth of the job is known, and the total points attached to it are converted into monetary values.

Table 1.3: Example of Point Method

S/NO	Compensable Factors	Driver	Clerk	Secretary	Receptionist	Typist
1.	Experience	3	2	4	3	3
2.	Skill	3	2	4	3	3
3.	Physical effort	3	2	2	2	2
4.	Mental effort	2	4	5	3	4
5.	Education	1	2	3	2	2
6.	Initiative	4	2	4	2	2
7.	Supervision	2	2	2	2	2
8.	Risk taking	5	2	3	2	2
9.	Difficulty	3	2	4	3	2
10.	Responsibility	3	3	4	3	2
	Ranking	2nd	4th	1st	3rd	5th

The point method offers a comprehensive and accurate method of job evaluation, with minimal prejudice because it places on the raters the need to investigate all key factors and sub-factors of a job.

Employees favor it because point values are assigned to all factors in a systematic way and account for differences in wages for various jobs based on the strength of the job factors. On the other hand, it is a complex, time-consuming, and expensive method that may be too taxing in evaluating managerial jobs where the nature of work is varied, complex, and novel, in such a way that it cannot be explained in quantifiable numbers.

Strategic Importance of Job Evaluation:

In the competitive landscape of talent acquisition and engagement, one of the fundamental tools that support this effort is strategic job evaluation. It is an asset in recruitment by providing clarity, fairness, and alignment in every stage of the hiring process so as to attract and retain the right people for the right roles. While many factors influence employee engagement, the role of job evaluation cannot be ignored; it plays a vital role in shaping how employees perceive fairness, recognition, and growth opportunities and, in turn, feel recognized, motivated, and connected to their work. The understanding of the importance of job evaluation will not only enhance recruitment and engagement but also extend to the overall organization's effectiveness in the following ways (Colin, 2022; El Balshy & Ismael, 2023; and Thandeka, 2025):

Influences on recruitment and selection:

In a market where talent is a key differentiator, organizations leverage on the information provided by job evaluation to conduct effective recruitment; since it furnishes detailed understanding of each job, it enables HR practitioners to craft precise and compelling job descriptions and helps builds trust and encourages high-quality applicants to engage with the organization, assess their fit and reduce mismatches during the hiring process. With well-defined job criteria, recruiters can more effectively identify the skills and qualifications needed, thereby aiding in the selection of suitable candidates, ensuring that the compensation offered is competitive and commensurate with the job's requirements (Heneman et al, 2018). What it means is that employees are chosen based on the prescribed competencies required in doing the job. Transparent and consistent job structures signal professionalism and fairness to candidates, and when the wages are competitive, they help to attract top talent and improve employer branding. Also, if everyone is on the same page as to which system is used to determine who gets the job, it eliminates discrepancies when selection results are published.

Influences on employee engagement:

The need to keep employees engaged with the company is one of the major responsibilities of HRM. When employees see that there is fair compensation and recognition based on job worth reduces resentment and fosters trust in management, or have clear roles with defined responsibilities and expectations, it reduces ambiguity, stress, and thereby boosts engagement (Milkovich et al, 2017). Recognition tied to job value and performance enhances morale and encourages discretionary effort, leading to improved engagement and retention, and making retained employee's essential members of the organization. Essentially, it creates a framework for career paths and promotions, helping employees to understand how their role fits into the broader organization- these are factors that foster engagement and strengthen commitment.

Influence on legal compliance:

Job evaluation involves analyzing job roles based on factors such as skills, responsibilities, effort, and working conditions, with the aim of creating a transparent framework for compensation, career progression, and organizational structure and effectiveness, in addition to serving as a strategic mechanism for ensuring legal compliance and minimizing employment-related risks. By providing a clear and objective basis for salaries and wages, job evaluation helps organizations align with labor laws and regulatory standards applicable in the state or country. For example, it supports the equal pay legislation in the US, namely the Equal Pay Act and Title VII of the Civil Rights Act, which is aimed at eliminating gender, racial, and other biases associated with compensation. The Equal Pay Act of 2010 guarantees that men and women in equal jobs earn equal wages. Job assessment offers evidence to support equal pay and reduces the risk of discriminatory hiring, promotion, and termination when organizations anchor their decisions on certain job criteria like skills, responsibilities, effort, and working conditions, rather than personal characteristics. The documentation of job evaluation criteria provides evidence of fair and consistent employment practices, which would be useful during audits by government agencies like the Department of Labor or EEOC, and safeguards the organization against potential legal and reputational damage. Beyond legal compliance, job evaluation improves documentation and accountability, strengthens employee trust, and enhances managerial consistency.

Influence on organizational change and adaptability: In today's dynamic workplace, companies must continuously evolve to remain competitive, and this has made change and adaptability a necessity, and job evaluation a much-desired tool for its accomplishment. By defining roles and their interrelationship, job evaluation serves as a strategic guide for organizational design or redesign. This role clarity is important when firms decide to restructure, merge, or expand their operation. For instance, new roles can be evaluated and assimilated into existing roles seamlessly to meet changing demands, which is vital if the organization must remain competitive and responsive in a fast-changing business environment. Similarly, in times of technological disruptions, job evaluation can assist organizations to quickly reassess and redefine roles, thus supporting rapid adaptation, without compromising internal equity. The agility of an organization to adjust to new conditions, learn new skills, and thrive amid uncertainty cannot be overemphasized in today's business world. Strategically, it facilitates workforce planning by aligning employees with the broader organizational strategies.

Furthermore, a well-structured delineation of responsibilities fosters better coordination across departments, reduces duplication of effort, and aligns all units toward shared organizational objectives. Evaluating roles carefully can help identify skill gaps and future workplace needs, and prompt necessary actions, too. For example, more resources may be allocated to positions that are crucial for achieving business goals. Organizations can use this insight to make investments in talent acquisition, reskilling of employees, training and development, and aligning talent with evolving business goals. Other areas where job evaluation information can be strategically applied are in designing career ladders and growth opportunities within the company, which, in turn, enhance employee engagement and development.

Workforce planning is the systematic process of analyzing current workforce capabilities and forecasting future talent needs, by balancing labor supply with demand, based on organizational goals (Lucija, 2025). CIPD (2025) defines it as a core process of human resource management that is shaped by the organizational strategy and ensures the right number of people with the right skills, in the right place at the right time to deliver short- and long-term organizational objectives. It requires organizations to analyze the current workforce in terms of availability, skills, and performance; identify future skill requirement; forecast talent supply and demand; and develop strategies to bridge the gap between the two, and such strategies may include hiring, upskilling, retention, and redeploying of employees (Marc, 2025; Elk, 2024; and SHRM, 2024).

For more details, the components of workforce planning would involve five factors, namely, workforce analysis. The analysis would assess the current workforce to understand its composition, skills, performance, and potential. Other analyses include employee demographics, turnover rates, and productivity levels. This is with a view to gaining insight into their workforce dynamics and, at the same time, identifying strengths, weaknesses, and areas that require development. The next factor is the demand forecasting, which predictively looks into the future workforce needs of the organization based on its strategic goals and business plans. It would estimate the number of employees and the types of skills required to meet future demands. Other factors to predict include market trends, technological advancements, and business growth projections, amongst others. Gap analysis is another crucial component of workforce planning, which compares the current workforce's capabilities with the future workforce requirements identified in demand forecasting. It provides a clear picture of the areas where the organization must invest its resources. Having identified the gaps, the next component revolves around developing an actionable plan (workforce planning strategies) to mitigate the gaps identified. These strategies may include recruiting external candidates to fill positions; using learning and development to enhance the skills of current employees to meet future needs; succession planning; and implementing initiatives to retain valuable employees and reduce turnover rates (employee engagement). The fifth factor is the implementation and monitoring, which requires coordination across various departments and continuous communication to ensure alignment with organizational goals. Regular reviews and updates help to keep the workforce planning process dynamic and responsive to changing business needs.

Effective workforce planning helps to align talent with both the short-term and long-term goals by balancing labor supply with demand. It is essential for aligning human resources with business goals, optimizing workforce performance, and preparing for future staffing needs. Workforce planning broadly covers two important areas- the operational, which is the short-term strategies to handle day-to-day challenges and changes; and the strategic, which is the long-term strategies of 3-5-A one-year time horizon that is focused on the organization's mission, vision, and goals.

The need for organizations to have the right people, in the right place, with the right skills at the right time is one that is frequently extolled in the HR community. In practice, workforce planning is to ensure you have the people resources in place to deliver the short-term and long-term objectives of your organization. Workforce planning as a subject of study comes under names like 'personnel planning', 'human resource planning', 'employment planning', or 'manpower planning.' In whatever name it comes, it is a strategic and systematic alignment of an organization's human capital with business direction. It is systematic in the sense that it involves analyzing the current workforce, identifying future workforce needs, establishing the gaps between the present an the future needs, and implementing solutions so that the organization can accomplish its mission, goals, and objectives. Some of the underlying theories and practices that inform this topic are human capital theory (posits that investment in people through education, training and healthcare increases their productivity and value to an organization); resource -based theory- that emphasizes need for HR to play a more proactive role in shaping business strategy; and people analytics- using data-driven insights to improve people-related decisions.

As a process of striking a balance between human resources required and acquired in an organization, it compares existing labor resources with the forecast of labor demand and the outlining of activities for acquiring, training, redeploying, and possibly discarding labor. The comparison will assist organizations to acquire the desired human resources in the right quality, right numbers, right places, and right times to successfully achieve their overall objectives. It is a process of identifying and responding to organizational needs and charting new policies, systems, and programs that will assure effective human resource management under changing conditions.

The ultimate objective of a workforce planning function is to determine how best to recruit, grow, deploy, optimize, and retain employees. However, workforce planning is no longer as simple as it used to be due to a number of complex factors that characterize the workforce of today. They come in the form of a global talent pool, a diverse nature of workers, employee engagement, high expectations on the part of employees, and the employer, etc. Meeting employees' needs and those of the organization is a difficult balancing task that HR must achieve. Effective workforce planning serves to act as the panacea for most employee/employer problems, such as turnover, low productivity, low engagement, misfits, low potential realization, etc. Workforce planning is a holistic process that takes inputs from other HR processes– recruitment, learning and development, employee engagement, career and succession planning, compensation, and benefits in aligning with organizational strategy.

Today, workforce planning has assumed strategic positions in organizations. The term strategic workforce planning (SWP) defines the alignment between human resources and the company's core business goals.

Workforce planning determines what an organization needs in terms of the size, type, experience, quality, skills, and knowledge of its workforce in order to achieve primary business goals. Strategic workforce planning (SWP) is critical because it helps maintain a focus on longer-term workforce development and business goals, so that it will not end up in a fire brigade approach to handling business issues. This powerful tool could cause significant change and, perhaps most intriguingly, truly align workforce planning activities with business goals. Business leaders get fired up over SWP because it brings everyone into alignment and builds focus around the same goals.

Strategic Importance of Workforce Planning:

Workforce planning is one of the most important issues in the field of human resource management that contributes to making organizations effective and efficient in their product or services (Anyadike, 2013). It helps minimize and, where possible, eliminate current and future staffing issues by ensuring organizations have the right people in the right roles at the right time. This is because today's business organizations must be agile, strategic, and forward-thinking to attract and retain top talent. The task of implementing workforce planning is daunting because it proactively manages talent, anticipates shortages, and makes informed decisions about hiring and development. It analyses the human resources of an organization, such as the aging workforce that can lead to talent shortages in certain areas due to mass retirement and a lack of appropriate skills; skills that can give the company a competitive edge; to hiring and keeping employees who are both ambitious and skilled, thereby creating an adequate pipeline for the long-term sustainability and success of an organization. Below are some areas that workforce planning can influence organizational outcomes (Sarah, 2025; David, 2025; Schroeder-O'Neal, 2025):

Enhances recruitment:

In today's competitive and rapidly evolving business landscape, strategic workforce planning has emerged as a cornerstone of effective talent acquisition. This proactive approach aligns staffing strategies with long-term organizational objectives, transforming recruitment from a reactive process into a strategic advantage. Rather than simply filling immediate vacancies, workforce planning enables HR professionals to forecast future talent needs based on anticipated growth, market trends, and technological shifts. This foresight allows organizations to recruit individuals who not only meet current requirements but also possess the potential to evolve with the company. Additionally, workforce planning helps HR teams identify and prioritize roles that are critical to strategic success, ensuring that recruitment efforts are focused on sourcing top-tier talent for high- impact positions. This targeted approach enhances the precision and effectiveness of recruitment campaigns, contributing to a more resilient and future-ready workforce.

Beyond strategic alignment, workforce planning strengthens recruitment outcomes by facilitating the development of robust talent pipelines. By anticipating future hiring needs and engaging potential candidates early, organizations can reduce time-to-hire and maintain continuity in key roles through succession planning and internal mobility. Moreover, workforce planning supports budget optimization by preventing overstaffing and understaffing, allowing resources to be allocated based on actual needs rather than reactive decisions. This reduces reliance on costly emergency hiring and improves overall recruitment efficiency. Organizations that demonstrate strategic foresight in their hiring practices are perceived as stable and forward- thinking, enhancing their employer brand and attracting high-quality candidates seeking long-term career growth. Ultimately, a well- executed recruitment strategy grounded in workforce planning not only improves talent acquisition but also boosts employee retention by aligning roles with individual aspirations and organizational goals.

Apart from recruitment, effective workforce planning serves as the cornerstone of an integrated talent management strategy. As organizations increasingly rely on high-caliber talent for managerial and professional roles, workforce planning helps address talent scarcity by guiding both internal development and external hiring. It enables businesses to anticipate future skill needs, adapt to technological change, and avoid critical talent shortages.

Through structured talent action plans, HR leaders can clearly define responsibilities and implement targeted strategies to attract, retain, redeploy, and develop the workforce needed to meet future demands. These plans typically **focus on three core activities:** recruiting capable individuals, nurturing key talent, and forecasting to close gaps between current capabilities and future requirements. Ultimately, workforce planning fosters a forward-looking culture, ensuring organizations are prepared for growth and resilient in the face of change.

Enhances employee engagement:

Workforce planning plays a vital role in enhancing employee engagement by ensuring that organizations have the right people, with the right skills, in the right roles, at the right time. When strategically implemented, it creates clarity around job expectations and organizational priorities, helping employees understand how their work contributes to broader goals. This alignment fosters a sense of purpose and belonging—two core drivers of engagement. Moreover, workforce planning enables organizations to anticipate future talent needs, which opens up opportunities for upskilling, reskilling, and internal mobility. Employees who see a clear path for career development are more likely to remain motivated, committed, and invested in the organization's success.

In addition to career growth, workforce planning contributes to a healthier work environment by balancing staffing levels and preventing both overstaffing and understaffing. This balance helps maintain manageable workloads, reducing burnout and increasing job satisfaction. Furthermore, when workforce decisions are based on data and communicated transparently, it builds trust between employees and leadership. Employees feel valued and respected when they are kept informed and when their roles are shaped by thoughtful planning rather than reactive measures. Ultimately, workforce planning is not just a tool for operational efficiency; it is a strategic lever for cultivating a more engaged, resilient, and high-performing workforce.

Alignment with business strategy:

Aligning workforce planning with business strategy ensures that talent decisions directly support organizational goals such as market expansion, digital transformation, product innovation, and operational efficiency. By translating strategic objectives into specific skill and role requirements, workforce planning enables organizations to prioritize tasks, allocate resources effectively, and maintain a unified direction across teams. When integrated with broader business planning, it allows companies to anticipate shifts in demand, respond swiftly to change, and guide talent acquisition and development with purpose. This proactive approach fosters cohesion and agility, helping organizations prepare for future needs through upskilling, succession planning, and internal mobility.

Strategic workforce planning also enhances operational resilience by forecasting talent needs based on growth projections, market trends, and succession pipelines. It identifies potential skill gaps before they become critical, enabling timely interventions through recruitment, training, or redeployment. This flexibility is especially vital in industries facing rapid technological disruption or market volatility. Moreover, aligning workforce planning with strategic priorities ensures optimal use of human capital investments, directing budgets and development efforts where they yield the greatest impact. The result is a more adaptive, cost-efficient, and growth-oriented organization equipped to navigate change and sustain long-term success.

Optimal business performance depends on the seamless coordination of equipment, supplies, logistics, and talent, and when any of these resources falter, operational efficiency suffers. The COVID-19 pandemic highlighted this vulnerability, as workforce shortages and supply chain disruptions significantly impacted production and delivery capabilities, even for companies with adequate staffing. Without a strategic workforce planning approach, organizations risk falling behind in a rapidly evolving landscape. As technology advances and the skill gap widens, businesses must proactively prepare to secure the talent needed for future growth. Failing to do so can lead to missed opportunities, reduced competitiveness, and long-term stagnation.

Supporting organizational learning and development: Workforce planning plays a pivotal role in supporting organizational learning and development by aligning talent strategies with future business needs and fostering a culture of continuous growth. At its core, workforce planning involves analyzing current workforce capabilities, forecasting future skill requirements, and identifying gaps that must be addressed to achieve strategic objectives. This process directly informs learning and development (L&D) initiatives by pinpointing the competencies that need to be cultivated across the organization.

By anticipating future talent demands, whether driven by technological change, market expansion, or evolving customer expectations, workforce planning enables HR leaders to design targeted training programs that build critical skills before they become urgent. It also supports succession planning by identifying high–potential employees and preparing them for leadership roles through structured development pathways. Furthermore, workforce planning encourages internal mobility by mapping career trajectories and ensuring employees have access to reskilling and upskilling opportunities.

This not only enhances employee engagement and retention but also ensures that the organization remains agile and competitive in a rapidly changing environment. Ultimately, workforce planning transforms learning and development from a reactive function into a strategic driver of long-term success.

Cost reduction:

Workforce planning plays a critical role in mitigating talent costs by aligning human capital strategies with business needs, optimizing resource allocation, and reducing inefficiencies across the employee lifecycle. Rather than reacting to staffing shortages or surpluses, strategic workforce planning enables organizations to anticipate future talent demands and proactively manage recruitment, development, and retention efforts. This foresight minimizes the need for last-minute hiring, which often comes at a premium due to urgency, limited candidate pools, and reliance on external agencies.

One of the most impactful ways workforce planning reduces costs is by preventing overstaffing and understaffing. Overstaffing leads to inflated payroll expenses and underutilized talent, while understaffing can result in overtime costs, burnout, and decreased productivity. Avoiding overstaffing or understaffing and optimizing the mix of full- time, part-time, and contingent workers are beneficial. This cost control is especially vital during economic downturns or periods of rapid expansion. By forecasting workforce needs based on business growth, market trends, and internal succession plans, organizations can maintain optimal staffing levels. Additionally, workforce planning supports internal mobility and targeted upskilling, reducing dependency on external hires and lowering onboarding and training expenses. It also helps HR teams prioritize critical roles and allocate recruitment budgets more effectively, ensuring that investments in talent yield maximum strategic value.

References

Anderson, V. & Caldwell, C. (2018). Job analysis: The building block of human resource management. Journal of Organizational Psychology.

https://www.researchgate.net/publication/322525643_Job_analysis_The_building_block_of_human_resource_management

Armstrong, M. (2012). Armstrong's handbook of human resource management Practice, (12th Edition), London, Koga Page.

Anyadike, N. O. (2013). Human resource planning in Nigeria public organization. Global journal of Human Resource Management, 1(4), 56-68.

Askarov, R (2024). Understanding job analysis: A comprehensive guide.

https://www.monitask.com/en/hr-glossary/job-analysis

Bhasin, H. (2021). Job Design–Meaning, Characteristics and Principles.

https://www.marketing91.com/job-design/

Colin, B. (2022). What is a job evaluation, and how do you conduct one?

https://leaders.com/articles/business/job-evaluation/

Coursera (2024). Why conducting a job analysis is important.

https://www.coursera.org/enterprise/articles/job-analysis

Cascio, W. F. (2018). Managing human resources: Productivity, quality of work life, profits.

McGraw-Hill Education. CIPD (2025). Workforce Planning.

http://www.cipd.org>news>guidance-workforce-planning CIPD launches practical guidance on workforce planning.

David, A (2025). The link between job design and employee health.

https://www.corporatewellnessmagazine.com/article/the-link-between-job-design-and-employee-health

Daniels, K., Gedikli, C., Watson, D., Semkina, A., & Vaughn, O. (2017). Job design, employment practices and well-being: A systematic review of intervention studies. Ergonomics, 60(9), 1177–1196. https://doi.org/10.1080/00140139.2017.1303085

Elk, S. (2024). Why Strategic Workforce Planning Is More Valuable Than Ever. Forbes. https://www.forbes.com/sites/selk/2024/08/27/why-strategic-workforce-planning-is-more-valuable-than-ever.

El Balshy, S. & Ismael, M. (2023). Job evaluation as a mechanism for achieving the fairness of a wage structure in the administrative system: Theoretical perspectives. Journal of Humanities and Applied Social Sciences, 5(1), pp. 3–19, doi: https://doi.org/10.1108/JHASS-02-2021-0038

Hackman, J. R. and Oldham, G. R. (1975). Development of job diagnostic survey. Journal of Applied Psychology, 60(2), 159-170.

Heneman, R. L., Judge, T. A., & Kammeyer-Mueller, J. D. (2018). Staffing organizations. Routledge.

Indeed (2025 a). The importance of performing a job analysis (with examples).

https://www.indeed.com/career-advice/career-development/jobs-analysis

Indeed (2025 b). Methods of job analysis (with definition, benefits, and uses).

https://www.indeed.com/career-advice/career-development/methods-of-job-analysis

Indeed (2025c). Job Design: Definition, importance and strategies.

https://www.indeed.com/career-advice/career-development/job-design

Irene et al (2025). Mapping the Literature on Job Evaluation: A Scoping Review. Compensation & Benefits Review, 57(1), pp.24-46. DOI: 10.1177/08863687241279592

Keeler, J. B., Brock Baskin, M. E., Lambert, A., Clinton, M. S., & Barger Johnson, J. (2022). Practicality of job analysis in today's world of work. Industrial and Organizational Psychology: Perspectives on Science and Practice, 15(1), 65–69.

https://doi.org/10.1017/iop.2021.128

Lucija, B. (2025). Workforce Planning Guide: Definition, Process, Strategies.

https://productive.io/blog/workforce-planning/

Marc, H (2025). What Is Workforce Planning? Definition, Practices, and Benefits.

https://www.netsuite.com/portal/resource/articles/huma-resources/workforce-planning.shtml

Milton. J (2025). What are the six steps of job analysis, and examples?

https://www.thehumancapitalhub.com/articles/what-are-the-six-steps-of-job-analysis-and-examples

Milkovich, G. T., Newman, J. M., & Gerhart, B. (2017). Compensation. McGraw-Hill Education.

Sarah, B. (2025). What is a Workforce Plan and Why Does It Matter?

https://www.staffcircle.com/blogs/what-is-a-workforce-plan/

SHRM (2019). Job analysis and job design.

https://www.shrm.org/resourcesandtools/tools-and-samples/toolkits/pages/jobanalysisandjobdesign.aspx

SHRM Labs. (2024). Strategic Workforce Planning: Navigating the Future of HR. SHRM.

https://www.shrm.org/labs/resources/strategic-workforce-planning-navigating-the-future-of-hr

Susanto et al (2024). Human resource management concepts: Recruitment, job analysis, job evaluation, remuneration, and organizational development. Greenation International Journal of Law and Social Science, 2(3), pp. 88-104. DOI: https://doi.org/10.38035/gijlss.v2i3

The Enterprise World. (2025). 7 Reasons Why Workforce Planning Is Important in 2025. https://theenterpriseworld.com/why-is-workforce-planning-important

Thandeka, M. (2025). What is The Importance of Job Evaluation for a Booming Company?

https://www.thehumancapitalhub.com/articles/What-Is-The-Importance-Of-Job-Evaluation-For-A-Booming-Company

Wonders, M. E., Hoover, A. N., Rupp, D. E., Kaplan, S., Strah, N., & Ratwani, K. (2025). The application of within-person methods to promote inclusive job analysis. Organizational Psychology Review, 0(0). https://doi.org/10.1177/20413866251333067

Schroeder-O'Neal, M. (2025, April 21). Strategic Workforce Planning: 3-Step Guide for CHROs. Gartner. https://www.gartner.com/en/articles/strategic-workforce-planning

Chapter Two: Recruitment

Definitions.

Recruitment and selection are two key terms in the hiring process and remain a major function in human resource management, usually assigned to the human resources department. Many definitions have been offered as to what constitutes recruitment. According to Rajyalaxmi (2023), it is the process of attracting qualified and competent personnel for different jobs, which includes the identification of existing sources of the labor market, the development of new sources, and the need for attracting many potential applications so that good selections may be possible. But Alzhrani (2020) asserts that the purpose of recruitment is to seek out or explore, to evaluate, to induce, and to obtain commitment from the prospective employees to fill positions required for successful operation and organization. In his book, Khanka (2007) describes recruitment as generating applications from applicants for specific positions to be filled in the organization. While Anjali and Anam (2022) view recruitment as the process of examining a vacant position in the organization and attracting potential candidates to apply for the same, within an appropriate time and at a desirable cost.

From the above definitions, we can say that recruitment is for searching and securing applicants for the various job positions that arise from time to time in the organization. The process of searching for prospective employees and stimulating them to apply for jobs in an organization is termed recruitment, and the process of choosing from among applicants who best meet the job criteria is known as selection. In other words, recruitment is concerned with attracting a large pool of individuals with the right profile in terms of qualification, experience, skills, and other relevant attributes to indicate their interest in working for an organization, and thereafter, selection commences.

Strategic recruitment and its role in organizational strategy:

In recent times, there has been a paradigm shift in the recruitment process, moving away from the traditional recruitment, which is reactive, responding to immediate hiring needs, and the filling of vacancies. Many organizations have adopted strategic recruitment in the anticipation of future manpower needs. It also helps them to be proactive, incorporating organizational changes and growth that may occur over time. Strategic recruitment addresses the manpower challenges, especially when an organization is looking forward to creating an ongoing pipeline of talent and building relationships with potential candidates. Hence, strategic recruitment has been defined as a planned process that aligns hiring practices with the organization's long- term goals (Goncalves, 2024). It involves planning, forecasting, and analysis to ensure that the right people are in the right position at the right time (Askarov, 2024). Proactive business concerns are using strategic recruitment as a tool for sustaining a competitive edge by analyzing future personnel needs and devising means to ensure that the talent needed to meet the long-term goals is always available. This, unlike traditional recruitment, is mainly concentrated on filling vacancies momentarily or as the need arises. The use of strategic recruitment requires a good understanding of the business goals and objectives, constant analysis of the trends in the labor market, and the ability to adjust strategies as needed. The key elements of strategic recruitment are highlighted below.

- Talent forecasting: Based on business goals and directions, organizations predict their future talent needs, anticipate market trends, and growth or changes within the organization.
- Employee branding: This is the image and reputation of an organization, a project for potential employees. It conveys your value, culture, and work environment. Hence, developing a strong employer brand to attract competent candidates would differentiate a company from its competitors.
- Candidate experience: There is a need to create an engaging and positive experience with job candidates throughout the recruitment process to enhance the company's reputation as an employer of choice.
- Data-driven decision making; Oftentimes, emotional

biases can cloud decision-making in the recruitment process, resulting in costly hiring mistakes. Therefore, to mitigate the risk, it is good to base hiring decisions on objective data, as this will lead to the selection of candidates who are a better fit.

- Diversity and inclusion: strategies that ensure a diverse and inclusive workforce will most likely bring varied perspectives and experiences to the organization
- Expand your reach: Top candidates are not confined to specific geographic regions, hence the need to expand your recruitment reach beyond borders by using appropriate information technology.

Recruitment is no longer transactional or a peripheral activity of the HR department; it has become strategic to the extent of influencing organizational performance and capability, culture, and competitive edge. Today, organizations are aligning recruitment with their strategy to ensure goal achievement and long-term sustainability. When recruitment is aligned with business frameworks like VRIO and Balanced Scorecards, it serves as an important competitive advantage in driving employee engagement, innovation, and organizational growth. Using the criteria outlined in VRIO, the human element of the organization is a source of asset that is valuable, rare, inimitable, and well-organized (Barney, 1991). Also, when recruitment is aligned to Balance Scorecard (Kaplan & Norton, 1992), it influences financial outcomes by reducing turnover cost and improving ROI, customer service outcomes by recruiting workforce with deep commitment and excellent customer service, recruitment support organizational internal processes, which fuels innovation and processes improvement by selecting job candidates with problem-solving expertise; and promotes learning and growth by sourcing individuals who contribute positively to the organization. The strategic aim of recruitment, therefore, is to move beyond filling vacancies towards building strategic capabilities for long-term survival of an organization, through every hire.

- Determine the present and future recruitment needs of the organization in conjunction with the human resource planning activity and the job analysis activity. This is the initial step of analyzing current manpower needs, with a view to estimating what may be required in the future, aligned with the company's business policy.
- Infuse fresh blood with a new perspective to add value to the organization.
- Increase the pool of job applicants with a minimum cost, which will help increase the success rate of the selection process by reducing the number of obviously unqualified or overqualified applicants.
- To develop organizational culture and values that attract competent people.
- Help reduce the probability that applicants, once recruited and selected, will leave the organization after a short period. This is because a good recruitment system allows companies to hire people who value their workplace culture, which positively impacts employee retention and job satisfaction.

- Meet the organization's responsibility for the affirmative action program and other legal and social obligations regarding the composition of its workforce.
- Start identifying and preparing potential applicants who will be appropriate candidates.
- Increase organizational and individual effectiveness in the short and long term. This is for when recruiters hire candidates, they try to connect with people who hold the competencies that could contribute to business initiatives and goals.
- Evaluate the effectiveness of various techniques and locations of recruiting for all types of job applicants.

Process of Recruitment:

Basically, the process of recruitment involves assessing the job, ascertaining the source of labor supply, and attracting applicants. The first step in recruitment is to determine the vacancies that exist. It needs to be established that vacancies really exist, and there is a need to fill the vacancies. Where it exists, human resource practitioners should avoid the so-called 'automatic replacement syndrome.' One of the best approaches when a vacancy occurs is to see if the job can be reorganized or rescheduled amongst existing job descriptions of current employees. Potential vacancies occur because of people either leaving an organization or because of expansion. When the organization has taken the option to recruit new employees, it must be able to determine if a vacancy exists by providing accurate answers to some questions, such as:

- What job needs to be done?
- Is it different from the ones the incumbents are doing?
- What are the role profile and person specifications for the job?
- What are the key aspects of the job that will be advertised to attract ideal candidates?
- Where will it be advertised? The HR recruitment policy of the company will dictate whether the job will be advertised to existing employees only or will be advertised in the external labor market.

Note that the job description, role profile, and person specification will be very useful in providing information with respect to several issues, such as the job and job title, the reporting relationships, objectives of the job, duties, and responsibilities, the key performance indicators, key competencies, etc. The information can be extended to include terms and conditions of the work, pay, benefits, and hours of work. Others may include special requirements such as mobility, traveling, learning and development, and career opportunities. Alternatively, when a vacancy occurs, and the organization does not want to embark on recruiting new employees, the most obvious strategy could be to use one or a combination of the following:

- Sub-contract the work in the form of outsourcing.
- Use overtime, thereby existing employees could work beyond the normal hours and at the same time earn more.
- Mechanize the work by introducing new technologies

that will give high output.

- Reorganize the job so that it is possible to encourage part-time work.

Sources of Recruitment:

The sources of recruitment can be broadly classified into internal and external sources as discussed below:

Internal sources:

Internal sources of recruitment mean that management is looking inward to hire from within the organization. The applicants are those who are currently employed within the same organization. It is a major source of recruitment in the sense that organizations are selecting candidates with whom they are familiar in terms of their capabilities and performance at work. When companies decide to recruit internally, the HR department will advertise the job position via a circular placed on the notice board and online portal, inviting employees to apply so that they can be interviewed. Internal recruitment comes with many advantages: first, the organization is dealing with people they know strengths and weaknesses, unlike strange people. Secondly, the idea behind internal recruitment provides an opportunity for better utilization of the talents available within an organization. Thirdly, it is cost-effective because the organization may not spend much money, time, and effort on the recruitment of potential candidates, and lastly, preferring existing employees to outsiders in terms of filling vacancies helps to boost their morale and commitment. Promotion through internal recruitment serves as a source of motivation for employees and helps them to retain competent staff. However, certain drawbacks have been identified: it may limit multi-dimensional talent from the vast labor market and may lead to inefficiency. Also, recycling old hands may limit fresh viewpoints from entering the organization. Furthermore, there is always conflict and controversy, whether vacancies are to be filled based on seniority or ability. Where ability becomes the determining factor, some senior employees may not be too happy working under their juniors who possess the ability required for the job. The internal sources of recruitment are highlighted thus:

- Present employees: This may come in different ways, for example, when a company decides to place an internal advertisement, and the job postings are open to all employees within the organization. It may also take the form of promotion, for instance, when a vacancy occurs, an organization may decide to move an employee from a lower position to a higher position, and this is usually accompanied by more responsibilities and remuneration. In addition, it can take the form of a transfer, which simply means swapping or interchanging employees depending on the requirements of the position.
- Former employees: Former employees who have good track records may wish to come back to the company on a part-time or full-time basis. This approach is cost-effective and allows organizations to recruit people they know of their competence.

- Employee referrals: The existing employees may wish to refer their friends to the organization as potential candidates to fill vacancies.
- Previous applicants: Previous applicants, whose applications are with the organization, may later be called upon to fill vacancies.
- People who are known to the manager: Obviously, one of the tasks of a professional manager is to continually be in touch with the professional community. A manager who belongs to some professional bodies and attends conferences and workshops is more likely to interact with lots of people who have what it takes to add value to his/her organization. They can be given an opportunity during the recruitment and selection processes.
- The direct approach by potential job candidates: If an organization has a reputation, it will receive lots of job candidates expressing their willingness to work for them. This is a type of Nigerian work environment where some candidates directly approach companies, not waiting to see and respond to their job adverts.

External sources:

This form of recruitment is targeted at candidates outside the organization. The aim is to attract prospective job seekers who are external to the organization and who would bring new ideas, innovation, creativity, and resourcefulness. Because it is an open process, a large number of applicants are attracted, making it possible to choose candidates with the requisite skills, knowledge, and abilities. Also, it provides healthy competition as the firm's doors are opened to other talented applicants who are ready to work with greater vigor and positive attitudes. There is no doubt that this may be expensive, but it has great potential for driving an organization towards the achievement of its goals. Recruitment from outside may create a sense of insecurity and demoralization among existing employees, who may be unwilling to share their institutional knowledge. External sources of recruitment include:

- Employment exchanges: These refer to government exchanges and executive registries located in strategic towns and cities. In some countries, it is managed by the Ministry or Department of Labor. The main functions of these employment exchanges are the registration of job seekers and their placement in the notified vacancies. Employers liaise with the employment exchanges in search of job candidates, who, in turn, pass on the names of suitable candidates to the employers.
- Employment Agencies: In addition to government agencies, there are some private employment agencies that register candidates for employment and furnish the list of suitable candidates from their database to prospective employers. They charge a fee or receive a percentage of the salary earned by the hired candidate during his first month or year. The main function of these agencies is to invite applications and shortlist suitable candidates for the organizations that need them, who make the final decision on the selection of the candidates. It is cheaper to go through employment

agencies than for organizations to recruit themselves, and it saves time that can be utilized in other productive activities. Most importantly, the organization remains unknown to applicants and reduces attempts to unduly influence recruitment or inundate an organization with applications.

- Professional Associations: When experts or people with special skills are to be recruited, Professional Associations can be contacted. Professional associations provide avenues to showcase their members (job seekers) in their journals and publications. Professional Associations are useful for attracting highly skilled and professional personnel.

- Campus recruitment: Some organizations visit schools and colleges on a recruitment drive. This form of recruitment is popular in American organizations. It used to be popular in many African countries in the early 60s up to the 80s, but when the economy of the nations started experiencing distress, its use declined substantially. Organizations interested in this type of recruitment visit institutions of higher learning to attract young engineers, scientists, and management trainees. This method of recruitment has some merits in the sense that the candidates are available in one place and interviews can be arranged at short notice. More so, it provides an opportunity to sell the organization to many graduating students.

- Deputation: This is the process of sending employees to another organization for a short period. For example, the Nigerian Government has been sending personnel in different areas of specialization to some West African countries, such as Gambia, Sierra Leone, Liberia, etc., for short-term services. It helps to provide expertise to organizations or countries that need it. They may not have to incur the initial cost of induction and training. However, due to the short period of time involved, the employees may not have had a significant impact on the organization that recruits them.

- Word-of-mouth: This method allows vacancies to be announced by word of mouth. This method of recruitment involves no cost, and one of its drawbacks is that the availability of candidates is restricted to a small number.
- Raiding or poaching: This is a method whereby rival firms offer better terms and conditions of service to attract another qualified employee from another firm to join them. It could be a challenge for human resources managers, whereby some good hands are recycled without the organization making concrete efforts to develop its members.
- Consultants: The recruitment of heads of departments and chief executives can be efficiently handled by search consultants. Bringing a new man to a top position may have an unsettling influence on existing staff; it may involve identifying and screening candidates outside with discretion. A good search consultant will have an excellent understanding of his/her client's challenges, the organizational objectives, and their future.
- Advertisement: This is the most widely used method of generating many applications. It involves the use of daily newspapers, trade journals, radio, television, the internet, etc. The main objective of an advertisement is to attract attention, create and maintain interest in the minds of job applicants, and stimulate action in the

applicants, who subsequently respond to the advertisement. The advertisement comprises vital information such as the name of the organization, the nature of the job, the competencies required, and the location of the company, a statement about salary, and how interested candidates should apply for the job.

- Newspapers Adverts: The choice of newspapers may be determined by the nature of work and the level of competence required. When organizations need people with specialized skills, it is advisable to advertise in national newspapers. But if they are semi-skilled workers they need, state or local newspapers may be ideal. Advertising jobs in the newspapers or the print media require a lot of creativity in the sense that the advert must generate interest, create an irresistible temptation, and prompt prospective job seekers to take immediate action. If the advert is well designed and the conditions of service attractive, this persuades prospective candidates, who ordinarily would not leave their present place of work, to consider it seriously.
- Television and Radio Adverts: Television and radio adverts are most likely to reach people who are not inclined to read newspapers, magazines, journals, etc. Also, radio and television are suitable when an organization wants to hire people urgently.

E-Recruitment:

This is a recruitment method that is online or web-based. It uses the company's public website or its own website to recruit staff. The process of e-recruitment involves attracting applicants, screening applications, tracking applicants, selecting, offering jobs, and rejecting candidates (Nishad & Anjali, 2019). The process is very straightforward: organizations put job vacancies on the internet (their own site or employment agency site), and interested candidates are encouraged to apply with their resume and curriculum vitae; names of applicants with relevant profiles are generated for the selection process. Companies that use e-recruitment stand to benefit in many ways because it is easier to process a large number of applications, including sending an acknowledgement to everyone who applied for the job. Apart from saving costs, it gives the impression that the company is up to date. The only shortcoming is that it is limited to candidates who have access to computers and good network systems, and might attract more job applicants than required. By extension, applicants may not derive the psychological satisfaction expected in human relations because they are dealing with machines that are already programmed.

Shortlisting:

Over time, there has been a debate as to whether shortlisting is a recruitment or selection activity. In this book, we shall treat it as a role that is shared between recruitment and selection processes. Every recruitment process is aimed at narrowing down the number of applicants to a manageable level, and therefore, it is like a funnel that gathers a large pool of candidates at the top and allows them to pass through a series of qualifying steps until the first round of applicants is shortlisted for an interview. Shortlisting can be a difficult task when the number of job applicants is extremely large. Shortlisting involves examining the information supplied by job applicants, sorting or sifting them, and drawing up a list of candidates to be interviewed. In this circumstance, it is professionally wrong to use some arbitrary method, such as age, sex, handwriting, etc., to reduce the number to a more manageable level unless they were mentioned in the advertisement. The steps will include careful examination of application and curriculum vitae or resume; processing the applications by listing them on the recruitment database (the database will contain information regarding the name of the applicant, date the application was received, whether it is rejected, kept on hold, short-listed for an interview, etc.) and coming up with short-listed names for the selection proper. When done manually, it will involve the use of a panel of managers to undertake the shortlisting exercise, with an agreed criterion for the shortlisting. The second approach involves the use of a software system that shortlists candidates electronically. This is possible where an online application is completed, which makes use of multiple-choice answers. With a well-defined criterion, such forms can be scored speedily and objectively. The candidates can also receive feedback immediately on whether they are successful or not. Then the successful ones can be invited to participate in the next stage of the recruitment process. Regardless of the method used, an efficient and effective shortlisting process will save time and money; enhance the experience for the hiring managers; improve the candidates' experience, and set some measurable standards for the hiring process (Moris, 2025).

Recruitment strategies:

A recruitment strategy is a formal plan of how organizations attract, identify, hire, and retain competent employees who would help them achieve their goals and add value to the bottom line. Depending on the type of business, any practice that is specifically designed to increase recruitment potential and effectiveness can be considered a recruitment strategy. A recruitment strategy should include recruitment planning, strategy development, recruitment criteria with regard to searching and screening of candidates, diversity and inclusion, employee and employer value propositions, etc. (Timpson, 2025). Some of the strategies are highlighted below:

- Recruitment planning: The first step is to outline the recruitment policies. You would want to know what role you need to fill (job description) and what the ideal candidate looks like (job specification), and mention of pay and other conditions attached to the job to be filled. It is always good to identify the roles you need to fill, their responsibilities, and the kind of candidates that would fill the positions (Armstrong, 2012:221). Furthermore, consider what your employer brand and culture have to offer in attracting the right candidates.
- Strategy development: Having done the planning, the next step is to devise a suitable strategy for recruiting

suitable candidates. The strategy includes decisions on the sources of recruitment, the geographical area to be covered, and other sequences of activities to undertake in the recruitment process.

- Searching: The third step involves attracting job seekers to the organization using both internal and external sources. This will also depend on the policy of a particular firm, the position of labor supply, government regulations, and agreement with labor organizations.
- Screening: Many authors see this as the starting point of selection. There is doubt about that; however, it is an integral part of recruitment. The fact remains that selection starts only when the applications have been screened and shortlisted. Screening uses job specifications. The bulk of applications at the preliminary stage are screened against the prescribed qualifications, knowledge, skills, and abilities in the preparation of the selection process.
- Evaluation and control: Finally, there is a need to look at the entire recruitment process to ascertain whether the recruitment process is cost-effective or not. If not, appropriate control measures can be introduced.

Employer/ Employee Branding:

Every organization has two sides to its brand- employer branding and employee branding. The concept of brand is used in the marketing of goods and services to potential customers, but has recently been adopted in the field of Human Resource Management. Employer branding is defined as the reputation an employer creates in the labor market, including its image that attracts prospective job applicants to associate with her. It is driven by the human resource team and top management of organizations who guide its brand, mission, and values, using some variables such as work culture, perks of office, and career advancement. On the other hand, employee branding is the perception created by employees and potential employees about a company as a workplace. It simply gets employees on board with the vision, mission, and values of an organization, so that they can help convey it to customers, stakeholders, and other employees. Employee branding is guided by the experiences of employees, who expressed their feelings about a particular company as to what they liked and, on their own, became brand advocates of the company (Kunsman, 2021; Urwin, 2022). No doubt, positive reviews from past and present employees play a crucial role in attracting prospective job candidates.

Both strategies synergize to make an organization attractive to job seekers so that the organization will become "employers of choice" in the labor market. It is what job applicants and customers think you are. To attract talent, the image of the company must be good. What it entails is that organizations should deliberately build a positive "brand image" over time, to the extent that potential employees will see it as highly desirable to work or associate with such an organization. Building a strong brand is essential for business success. Branding a consumer product is aimed at giving a distinctive feature that will differentiate it from others in the market. The same goes for employer branding. Some organizations or employers of labor have been identified by prospective employees as an organization that:

- Pay is relatively high, with a generous benefits package.
- Have flexible working hours.
- Job security.
- The work environment must be very good.
- Top management is known for its excellent ethical conduct.
- Work processes and systems must make headlines every now and then.
- The company must be selling its name like every consumer brand.
- Good learning and development programs, etc.

With these, an organization would be able to translate into a unique selling proposition or employee value proposition (EVP), which propels their communication when dealing with potential and actual applicants. According to Armstrong (2012:39-40) employee value proposition consists of what the company offers to its prospective and existing employees that they will value and appreciate, and which will persuade them to remain with an organization. It is the deal between the organization and the employee it is seeking to recruit and encompasses the value a company offers to its employees in return for the value they bring to the organization (what the employee expects of the company and what the company expects of the individual employee). The employee value proposition can be expressed as an employer brand in the sense that while EVP is an internal promise of the rewards employees will receive, the employer brand is how to market the value proposition externally to job seekers. Essentially, it is a way of differentiating from competitors and therefore becomes more appealing to candidates in terms of their needs, values, and wants. The aim is to make the organization 'an employer of choice'– that is to say, a company majority of people will prefer to work for and stay longer with.

Diversity, Equity, and Inclusion:

As the world becomes a global village, organizations are discovering values and opportunities in Diversity, equity, and inclusion (DEI). It has become a critical pillar of corporate resilience as companies create a business climate where people feel respected, valued, and enabled to make contributions. Many employers showcase their DEI in recruitment materials and job advertisements. The message they convey is that an organization welcomes the principle of diversity, where individuals from different backgrounds and perspectives can participate, including those from underrepresented groups. In other words, it means the organization employs people of various genders, races, ages, and sexual orientations. When they talk about equity, they are simply saying that they grant equal access to all participants in a fair and impartial manner. For example, it shows that the company offers equal opportunities, fair compensation, and balanced training and development opportunities. By extension, their inclusion strategy may consist of creating an environment where everyone has a sense of belonging, feels welcomed, respected, and accepted.

According to Shanken (2025), DEI comes with many benefits, especially around enhanced innovation. This is achieved by pulling together a wide range of perspectives, ideas, and experiences. A diverse workforce leads to improved decision-making, creativity, and innovation. They tend to be good at solving problems and making decisions by looking at issues from different directions. DEI initiatives have the propensity to attract and retain many employees because working in an inclusive workplace can boost employee satisfaction and therefore lower the rate of turnover. Also, firms that value DEI would be able to reach diverse customers, improve performance, and enhance their competitive edge.

Recruiting a more diverse workforce:

Recruiting a more diverse workforce requires consideration of several issues; some examples are given below:

- Gender Issues: It is important to understand how both men and women view managerial positions. In the early days, men predominantly held managerial jobs, and as a result, those jobs were viewed as primarily masculine in nature. Such stereotyping of management positions and their incumbents produced negative reactions to women in management, thereby inhibiting women from choosing or being chosen for managerial positions. While gender issues may not be much problem in the Western world, in some of the African countries, it still determines the positions one holds in offices. From the works of Schein (1973:95-100; 1975:340-344), it is abundantly clear that stereotyping has implications for gender issues in management. Also, it is easy to see how this can be transferred from gender issues to race, and so on. The lesson for human resource managers is to maximize the potential in both men and women. It is no longer whether you are a man or a woman, but whether you possess the necessary skills and abilities required in the modern place of work.

- Single Parents: Recruiting single parents and keeping them requires understanding the problems they encounter and how to balance them with work and family life. It will require making the workplace friendlier. Hence, it will be proper for organizations to have flexible work schedules and child-care benefits for single parents. Furthermore, there is a need to educate managers and supervisors to develop a supportive attitude towards supporting single parents in a virtual environment.

- Older workers: In Nigeria today, the age of service for some categories of workers has been elongated. For example, in the Judiciary, judges can now serve up to the age of seventy (70). The same goes for university lecturers. There is likely to be more agitation from other civil servants for the opportunity to continue in service even in their old age. Human Resource Managers should begin to think ahead of the challenges of managing older workers. Such challenges include:

- Provision of adequate medical facilities to cater to the health problems associated with older workers.
- Using younger supervisors to supervise the work of older workers, who may be older by twenty (20) or thirty (30) years, may be a challenge, given our cultural backgrounds.
- Training supervisors and managers to address age bias in the workplace.
- There may be a need for flexibility in work schedules so that those who cannot work full-time may have the option of working from their homes on a part-time basis.
- The disabled: There is still discrimination among disabled persons across the globe when it comes to the issue of recruitment. The Private Sector Organizations are the worst in this. Fair opportunities need to be given to the physically challenged people in job recruitment and selection. But rejection through ignorance can be very painful, especially when the disabled person knows that the employer is trying to imagine how he/she could cope rather than accepting his/her skills and experience. (Ododoru, 2007:18) However, employers need to change their attitudes to tap the huge potential in disabled persons. Disabled employees can provide organizations with excellent services in jobs ranging from information technology to creative advertising to receptionists. Deaf people can be very hard workers as they have few distractions. Employers offering appointments to disabled persons should assist them to settle down and cope with the challenges of the job. Office accommodation and arrangements may have to be altered to make it suitable for them. There may be a

need for elevators in tall buildings and special tables and chairs to ease their movement and work in the office. Blind people may need Braille software and may be allowed to use their guide dogs.

- Workplace inclusion of LGBTQ employees: One of the important considerations in the process of recruitment is the inclusion of lesbian, gay, bisexual, transgender, and queer (LGBTQ) employees as part of the workforce, thereby creating an environment where all employees will contribute to organizational goals and, at the same time, have a sense of belonging. It does not mean that all employees must agree with each person's lifestyle, but there should be respect for everyone's sexual orientation. The responsibility of companies is to establish a culture that appreciates LGBTQ and other minority groups and insists that they are fairly treated. To this extent, some organizations have defined appropriate workplace behaviors that are consistent with their diversity inclusion policy and now accommodate the LGBTQ by using an individual's preferred name and pronouns such as he/him, she/her, they/them, ze/hir, etc. They are also encouraged to speak up when they are not treated respectfully or discriminated against (Gonzales, 2022).

Organization's viewpoint on recruiting:

At least three factors affect recruitment from the organizational point of view. These include the set requirements, organizational policies and procedures, and organizational image. Organizations usually specify the requirements they think an ideal candidate should possess in each situation. Sometimes these expectations are so high that they become unrealistic. To minimize this kind of scenario, organizations should concentrate on the specifications that are necessary for the performance of the job. Organizations are also aware that job applicants are interested in knowing what an organizational policy is on several issues, such as career development, rewards, promotion, etc., hence many organizations strive to put some policies in place, not only for the effective management of the firm but also for attracting talent. Another important factor that organizations pay serious attention to is their image and reputation. The question of what the public, including prospective job candidates, thinks of the organization matters to every management. This is important for higher–level recruitment and in specialized fields. An organization's image is complex. It is based on what the organization does and whether it is perceived by job candidates as providing a good place to work. Usually, large organizations are more likely to have a good image, which they have built over the years by adopting best practices.

Job candidate's viewpoint of recruiting:

Having examined the viewpoints of organizations in recruiting, there are many factors that influence candidates' choice of organizations. These include the applicants' abilities, aptitude, and preferences based on the experience of friends and influences by parents, teachers, and other people they came across. These factors influence prospective job applicants in how they set their job preferences and how they go about seeking a job. Just as organizations set their requirements high when recruiting, applicants also have high expectations in terms of the conditions of work. Sometimes these expectations are not fulfilled. They also face the limits imposed by the labor market, government, labor unions, and organizational policies and procedures. Some individuals choose their occupation and the industry to work early in life. They back this up with relevant education and training. It has been observed that more educated candidates have a better knowledge of the labor market, higher expectations of the work conditions, and find organizations that pay more and offer stable employment.

Current trends shaping recruitment and selection:

Recruitment and selection are at the heart of building an agile, competent workforce capable of driving organizational goals and objectives, and hence, human resource practitioners and scholars must keep tabs on current and emerging issues that affect the recruitment and selection processes. Recruitment and selection have gone beyond attracting job seekers to fill vacancies but have become so strategic in meeting the long-term goals of organizations in terms of creating talent pipelines, driving innovation, and beating competition. The recruitment landscape has continued to evolve and will remain at the core of successful talent acquisition strategies. (Fitzpatric, 2025; Schindl, 2025). Let's explore the current trends redefining the scope of recruitment and selection:

Artificial Intelligence (AI):

AI has evolved and will continue to play a significant role in the recruitment and selection processes. It is the use of technology, aimed at recreating human cognitive skills, in addition to the ability to anticipate and account for potential problems (Rathore, 2023). These are machine learning models that can assist in shortlisting candidates, automate manual tasks, and streamline recruitment and selection workload, and free HR practitioners from repetitive hiring procedures. AI can analyze resumes, screen job candidates, predict cultural fit, speed up the recruitment process, and, in a more accurate manner, even reduce biases (Bholane, 2024; Chawla, 2024). AI has not only changed the functions of recruitment and selection but has also made it more efficient, with the ability to swiftly locate qualified candidates and match them with job descriptions as well as person specifications, thereby achieving the greatest possible fit. It is adding value through automation of processes, using science and data to enhance decision– making, and above all, acting as an intelligent agent or a chatbot in supporting business strategies. Today, it has provided a platform where employers and prospective job seekers connect and network online, hence facilitating online application submission; offering automatic responses; preliminary screening of resumes; checking social media pages of candidates for more detailed information; and scheduling of virtual job interviews (Nishad & Anjali, 2019).

Gamification in Recruitment:

This is a strategic approach to recruitment when compared with the traditional method. It involves some game elements and mechanics in the recruitment process, with a view to enhancing engagement, motivation, and participation of job candidates, and efficiency of the overall hiring process. A variety of activities can be employed, such as the use of game design techniques like points, badges, leaderboards, problem-solving, simulations, and other activities that create an atmosphere of interaction and promote an enjoyable experience for job applicants. The strategy can be used to evaluate candidates' skills and ability to handle challenges. By adding games to a non-game context, it lightens the recruitment space, reducing stress and making the whole process effective. This is because the interviewing process can be tedious for both job seekers and recruiters alike, hence the need to move away from the traditional recruitment to a more dynamic and engaging process. When applied properly, it can help to reveal whether applicants can demonstrate a wide range of competencies in the future, with respect to imagination, creativity, determination, resilience, and reasoning ability (Fitzpatrick, 2024; Schindl, 2025; Bholane, 2024). Furthermore, a study reveals that more the 78% of job candidates believe that some sort of gamification in a recruitment process makes a company more desirable (TheTalentGame, 2025). This strategic approach transforms how organizations attract, assess, and engage prospective candidates (Hure, 2025; SHRM, 2025).

Skill-based Hiring:

Employers are gradually shifting emphasis from degrees and formal education to skill-based hiring. In the years to come, recruitment managers will focus more on candidates' experience and soft skills. In fact, employers have come to realize that practical skills and relevant experiences outweigh academic credentials.

Emotional Intelligence:

Emotional Intelligence (EI) has become a cornerstone for effective recruitment in a rapidly changing and competitive job market. The recruitment landscape is leveraging EI in establishing meaningful and enduring connections with job candidates. EI is the ability to understand, manage, and utilize emotions in oneself and others and comprises self-awareness, self-regulation, empathy, and effective interpersonal skills. Since recruitment involves continuous interaction with job applicants, EI helps recruiters in interpreting responses from job seekers, managing their interactions, and regulating the recruiters' emotions. With EI, recruiters can navigate the complex emotional terrain of the hiring process and establish a deeper connection with applicants. It goes beyond evaluating skills and qualifications to identify candidates who are the best fit for the company's culture and values. EI brings several benefits to the recruitment processes, as highlighted below:

- Through interaction and effective communication, recruiters can understand the motivations, values, preferences, needs, and aspirations of job seekers and communicate in ways that resonate with them, leading to improved candidates' experience and trust. It also enhances the possibility of finding the right fit for the job.
- Recruiters with EI skills can easily adapt to changing scenarios by adjusting their strategies and approaches to meet new challenges and take advantage of emerging opportunities.
- Self-awareness supports ongoing self-development and growth, when recruiters recognize their strengths and weaknesses, thus enabling them to refine their skills.
- Applying empathy in the recruitment process is crucial in understanding candidates' perspectives, navigating conflicts, addressing concerns, negotiating effectively, and fostering harmonious relationships. Empathy is especially useful during stressful moments of the hiring process, such as contract negotiation.
- Since the recruitment process can be very demanding, recruiters with EI skills can manage stress and maintain a positive outlook, even in the face of challenges.
- EI empowers recruiters to balance the interests of the candidates and those of the company, as well as set healthy boundaries in their interactions. For example, recruiters can make choices that uphold the interests of all parties involved and are well equipped to say "no" when necessary.

References

Alzhrani, A. M. (2020). The Effectiveness of E-Recruitment Software over Other Online-Based Recruitment Methods.

Global Journal of Economics and Business, 8(2), 330–336.

https://doi.org/10.31559/GJEB2020.8.2.12

Anjali, K. & Anam, S. (2022). A Study on recruitment & selection practices at Accenture India Pvt. Ltd.

International Journal of Creative Research Thoughts, pp.10 (5). www.ijcrt.org

Armstrong, M, (2012). Armstrong handbook of human resource practice, London, Kogan page.

Askarov, R. (2024). Strategic recruitment.
https://www.monitask.com/en/hr-glossary/strategic-recruitment

Barney, J. B. (1991). Firm resources and sustained competitive advantage.

Journal of Management, 17(1), 99–120. https://doi.org/10.1177/014920639101700108

Bholane, K. P. (2024). Recent trends in recruitment and selection.

Journal of Organizational management, 78-86. https://www.researchgate.net/publication/374847587

Chawla, V. (2024). Latest trends in recruitment: Shaping the future of talent acquisition.

https://www.linkedin.com/pulse/latest-trends-recruitment-shaping-future-talent-vikas-chawla-mpdnc/

Fitzpatrick, K. (2025). New recruiting trends 2025.

https://www.ringover.com/blog/recruitment-trends

Goncalves, P (2024). The strategic recruitment process and its impact on achieving organizational objectives: Bibliographic review. Journal of Business and Management, 26(10).

Hure, D. (2025). How to use gamification in talent acquisition.

https://rewardtheworld.net/how-to-use-gamification-in-talent-acquisition/

Kaplan, R. S., & Norton, D. P. (1992). The balanced scorecard. Measures that drive performance. Harvard Business Review, 70(1), 71–79.

Kunsman, K. (2021). Reengineering the recruitment process. Harvard Business Review, March–April.

https://hbr.org/2021/03/reengineering-the-recruitment-process

Moris, A. (2025). Shortlisting: Best practices for employers.

https://www.davidsonmorris.com/shortlisting/

Nishad, N. and Anjali, M. G. (2019). Artificial Intelligence Chatbots are New Recruiters. International Journal of Advanced Computer Science and Applications, 10(9), pp.1-5.

Rathore, S. P. S. (2023). The impact of AI on recruitment and selection processes: Analyzing the role of AI in automating and enhancing recruitment and selection procedures.

International Journal for Global Academic & Scientific Research, 2(2), 78-93. https://doi.org/10.55938/ijgasr.v2i2.50

Rajyalaxmi, M. (2023). Human resources: Recruitment and selection processes.

International Journal of Novel Research and Development, 8(10), 118-132. https://www.ijnrd.org/papers/IJNRD2310213.pdf

Schein, E. H. (1973). Professional Education: Some New Directions. New York: McGraw-Hill.

Schein, E. H. (1975). How to change culture in organizations. In Organizational Psychology (2nd ed., pp. 287–307). Englewood Cliffs, NJ: Prentice-Hall.

Schindl, M. (2025). Recruiting trends 2025: What companies need to know now?

https://www.schulmeisterconsulting.com/en/magazine/overview/detail/recruiting-trends-2025-what-companies-need-to-know-now

Shanken, F. (2025). Why DEI Matters in America, and Who Benefits the Most.

https://phillywnc.org/why-dei-matters-in-america-and-who-benefits-the-most/

SHRM (2025). Recruiting executives benchmarking: Insights to maximize recruitment.

https://www.shrm.org/content/dam/en/shrm/research/2025-recruiting-benchmarking-report.pdf

Timpson, D. (2025). Crafting effective recruitment strategy and processes.

https://www.thomas.co/resources/type/hr-guides/effective-recruitment-guide

The Talent Game (2025). Gamification in recruiting: Everything you need to know.

https://thetalentgames.com/gamification-in-recruiting/

World Economic Forum's Future of Jobs Report (2025).

https://reports.weforum.org/docs/WEF_Future_of_Jobs_Report_2025.pdf

Chapter Three: Selection

Definitions:

Selection is the process of evaluating and interviewing candidates and selecting the right person for the right position (Pshdar et al, 2021). It is a process through which those who are recruited to serve as candidates are winnowed down to the few who are hired. Hence, they can be seen as a resource that can be distinguished from the recruitment pool that best meets organizational requirements for employment. It means the most suitable candidates, in terms of adjudged job- performance potentials, are picked from the available pool of applicants. Kapur (2018) views selection as the process of hiring employees among the shortlisted candidates and providing them with a job in the organization. Sakun (2022) defines selection as the process of selecting the most appropriate person who can fill the relevant job vacancy and deliver a valuable contribution to the entity.

Selection is simply the hiring of the best candidates from the pool of applicants (applications). It is an exercise in prediction and involves a process of picking the most suitable candidates from the applications received through recruitment to fill various jobs in the organization. It must be said that selection is more than choosing the best job applicants, but an attempt to strike a balance between what the applicants can do and what the organization requires. After shortlisting has been completed, the next step is to carry out selection, which may involve a combination of methods, summed up in the test and non-test methods. The thin line of difference between recruitment and selection is hinged on the fact that recruitment is the attraction of a pool of candidates for declared vacancies, while selection, on the other hand, and is the identification of the most suitable candidates for the job vacancies. The whole process of recruitment and selection is only completed when a job offer is generated and given to the best candidates by means of an appointment or letter of offer. Every selection method aims at providing evidence on which to base selection decisions. The decision is whether the job candidate can do the job. The evidence generated must be relevant and reliable. However, the most guaranteed evidence is to see the candidate do the job in such a way that elevates the success of the organization. When the selection process enables an organization to place the right candidates in the right jobs, the company enjoys the benefit of productivity and efficiency.

The effectiveness of any selection process largely depends on the quantity and quality of the candidates the organization can attract. For example, if the pool of candidates is too small, the organization is forced to hire from that pool, thereby increasing hiring mistakes. It is always better to hire from a large pool of candidates. But even when the best applicants are hired, it behooves the organization to create a conducive environment under which the employees can maximize their performance. The performance of the employee would be determined by several factors, such as competence and motivation levels; the extent to which they value their jobs and their commitment, and, most importantly, the leadership of the company.

There is no guarantee that any selection process will be one hundred percent effective, even when there is a conducive environment. Hiring mistakes abound, but what an effective selection process does is reduce the margin of error. It is for this reason that manager's offer probation periods, a time during which managers can further verify whether new recruits can demonstrate competence and good performance on the job. Sometimes, after probation, a new employee can be disengaged if he/she is not organizationally fit. Hence, selecting candidates who are organizationally fit would entail that recruiters would not only focus on individual behavior but also consider the context in which the behavior would be conducted.

Selection Methods/Processes:

Employee selection methods or processes are the efforts and techniques we employ in identifying, screening, and hiring suitable candidates for vacant positions (Kaushik, 2025). During the process, recruiters make tough decisions to ensure that successful candidates are appropriately vetted before getting hired. Effective employee selection methods are crucial to building a strong and agile workforce. This is accomplished by ensuring that there is a match between the job and the candidates' skills and abilities, which reduces the likelihood of mismatches and, in turn, decreases the rate of employee turnover. Hence, the primary goal of any selection process is to help select candidates with the right skills and ability to perform the job effectively; those that will align with company culture and create a more cohesive environment; and those that have the potential to grow and contribute to the company's long-term goals (Towers Perrin, 2003). There are different methods of selection, but the use can vary from organization to organization and depending on the type of role you are hiring. However, the combination of different methods affords companies the opportunity to hire the best candidates from the pool of applicants. What it means is that recruiters can use multiple methods in evaluating the suitability of job seekers for a particular role, by providing a 360-degree view of their competence level (Schmidt and Hunter, 1998). Some of the standard selection methods are discussed below:

Interviews:

An interview is a process of private conversation between two or more people, where questions are asked, and answers are received. The aim of every job interview is to examine and acquire information about the behavior, communication abilities, and competencies of the interviewee. An interview on a face-to-face basis, where the interviewer(s) engage the interviewee in a dialogue, or by phone. It can also be in the form of video interviews via Zoom, WhatsApp, or Skype. Generally, the interview process can further be broken down into a preliminary interview, a selection interview, structured and unstructured interviews, among others.

A preliminary interview usually follows screening; part of that recruitment process is already discussed in the previous chapter, the purpose is to eliminate unsuitable or unqualified candidates from the selection process. In the screening exercise, unqualified candidates are eliminated based on the information given in the application form, whereas the preliminary interview rejects misfits for reasons that did not appear in the application forms.

After the preliminary interview comes the selection interview. The aim of the selection interview is to establish the extent to which an individual will be able to do the job. The interview offers the opportunity to scrutinize the competence of a candidate in terms of skills, knowledge, and abilities, in line with the person specification, which had been prepared at the beginning of the recruitment. This involves face-to-face interaction between the interviewee and interviewer. It helps to secure the maximum amount of information from candidates about their suitability for the jobs under consideration. The objectives of the interview can be summarized thus:

- It confirms information already given by the candidate especially that in the application form or the test conducted.
- Additional information can be obtained from applicants, especially those that are not available in the application form, for example, certain qualities like manners, appearance, conversational ability, family background, etc.
- Facts about the job and organization are made available to the interviewee.
- The company can market its brand with the view to building trust and mutual understanding between the company and the applicant.
- It affords the opportunity of determining whether the job applicant will be culturally fit into the organization and how both parties will continue to get on together (Cai, 2023).
- Regarding unstructured interviews, they come in the form of a general discussion. The job candidate is asked several questions that are aimed at ascertaining his/her competencies for the job applied for. The panel of interviewers asks their questions at random, without any specific aim in mind, other than getting an overall picture. The predictive validity (the extent to which it predicts performance on the job) of the unstructured interviews is low. The most preferable method is the use of a structured interview, which, if carried out properly, has a higher level of predictive validity (Armstrong, 2012:230).
- However, a structured interview is one anchored on a defined framework, with a predetermined set of questions. Every job candidate for the same job is asked

the same questions and scored with a rating form. A structured interview is also suitable for the panel of interviewers who are focusing on the required behavioral competencies as set out in the person specification. Although structured interviews address most of the deficiencies of the unstructured interviews, they, in turn, suffer from the following weaknesses:

- It does not allow the interviewer(s) to change direction and address unanticipated issues during the interview because it is highly structured and pre-planned, and hence, lacks flexibility.
- It is limited and lacks validity as a means of making sound predictions of candidates' good performance on the job.
- It also lacks reliability in the sense of measuring the same thing for different candidates.

Figure 3.1: Sample of Structured Interview Rating Form

STRUCTURED INTERVIEW RATING FORM

location	
Post applied for	

1. <u>PERSONAL DATA OF INTERVIEWEE</u>:

Name: ………..…………………………………………………………………………

Sex: ……………………………

Date of Birth: …………………………………………...

Marital Status: ………………….

Phone No: ………………………………………..

State of Origin: ………………………………………………………………

Qualifications with date: ……………………………………………………………

Contact: ……………………………………………………………………………

Address: ……………………………………………………………………………

Residential Address: …………………………………………………………

2. <u>RECORD OF SCORES</u>:

	RECORD OF SCORES	MAXIMUM SCORE %	CANDIDATE'S SCORE %
A	Appearance/Physical Fitness	5	
B	Disposition/Eagerness and Confidence	5	
C	Ability to Communicate/Read (Verbal/Oral)	5	
D	Relevant Educational Qualification	10	
E	Relevant Experience	10	
F	Relevant Knowledge of The Job	45	
G	General Knowledge	10	
H	Estimate of Intelligence	10	
	TOTAL MARK	100	

3. Rater's

General Comment………………………………………………………………………

Signature: …………………… **Name**……………… **Designation**   **Date**……

Group interviews:

Group interviews assess (interviews) many candidates at the same time, observing how they interact, share ideas, and work together in a team. It is used to predict how groups may work in teams, resolve conflicts, and highlight leadership potential. This kind of interview can be used where the job duties are clearly defined and where many candidates can be informed and/or asked about the job requirements. Many types of interviews can be categorized under group interviews.

Another type of group interview is called a panel interview. This involves more than one interviewer, providing a diverse perspective on the suitability of a job seeker. It is usually a combination of individuals who are experts in their field. Since the evaluation is from a group of interviewers, it captures a holistic assessment of the candidate's skills and cultural fitness, thereby promoting fairness and mitigating the risk of subjective bias.

Fishbowl interviews also fall under group interviews. This type of interview is usually interactive because it brings several job applicants together to work with each other in a real-life setting. In another way, job seekers can be paired with staff members to work on a true-to-life issue. With this interview, recruiters can observe how individuals work and identify their skills regarding conflict resolution, problem-solving, analytical skills, and natural abilities as leaders and team players.

On a general note, group interviews save the recruiters' time, as well as that of the applicant. However, it can be threatening to some candidates, and in this regard, recruiters must help them loosen up and participate effectively. Since it involves more than one interviewer, each of them must have a defined role assigned before the commencement of the interview. Sitting arrangement is very important, and to help candidates feel free, most of the seats are circular or curve-patterned. It acts as a living room style to keep the interview more conversational and free-flowing.

Behavioral Interviews:

The premise of behavioral is that past job performance is the best predictor of future performance. In other words, the focus is on the applicants' work experience and behaviors to predict future performance. The questions revolve around past incidents that the candidate handled, to determine if his/her behavior and skills would align with the new role. The interviewer would be interested in proving how the candidate handled past job-related situations. For example, if an organization wants to fill a sales manager position, a question like this may be asked: "Can you tell us how you performed as a sales manager in your previous position with your company?" The answer the interviewer would be expecting is those that revolve around:

- Description of the situation or task and how the task is

completed

- Actions taken to see that it is completed
- The result or outcome of the assignment.

Assessment Centers:

Assessment centers provide a good opportunity to ascertain which candidates match the culture of an organization. This is a sophisticated assessment method that involves the use of several tools to assess candidates across a range of job-related situations. It uses a wide range of tests and structured interviews. The different tools used in the assessment center include simulations, ability tests, analysis, presentation, interviews, fact-finding exercises, group exercises, work samples, a test of productive thinking, etc. (Kleinmann and Ingold,2019). Assessment Centers have a high validity coefficient ranging from 0.37-0.45, which is an indication of their effectiveness in predicting job performance (Hermelin, eta al, 2007). It provides a comprehensive evaluation of candidates' competencies and allows employers to assess the competencies that fit the job role. With this, well-informed decisions are made, ensuring that new hires have the necessary skills to excel in their duties. Only very few organizations make use of assessment centers, especially the professional recruitment consultants and multinational corporations. The main objectives for the use of Assessment Centers include:

- It enables recruiters to focus on key elements of the job.
- It avoids over-reliance on a single technique.

- It is participatory and helps to bring out the best in the candidates.
- It is a good predictor of performance.
- It focuses on behavior.
- Several assessors or observers are used to avoid errors or bias. The aim is to increase the objectivity of assessment.
- Several candidates are assessed together.
- Several job-related circumstances are covered.

The disadvantage of this method is that it is very costly to set up and very time-consuming in implementation.

Stress interview:

This kind of interview gives an interviewer an opportunity to assess how well a candidate can cope with difficult situations. It can take different shapes. Sometimes difficult questions are asked, for instance, a question like "how many birds fly south for the winter?" and the interviewers would listen to the candidate's responses as well as his composure. On the other hand, the interviewers may even show some aggressive behavior to the applicant, which can cause the candidate to feel uncomfortable. The aim is to see how the candidate would react to such a situation. A stress interview tries to simulate a high-pressure working environment, and if a candidate is made uncomfortable in the process of the interview, he/she may not be a suitable candidate for that job. One of the advantages of this kind of interview is that it allows recruiters to observe firsthand the patience and resilience of candidates. It predicts candidates' ability to cope with pressure. On the flip side, it may lead to a poor experience and is capable of making some candidates upset. A candidate who felt mistreated during the interview process may share such negative feelings on social media, which may not augur well for the image of the company.

Data Analysis:

This refers to the use of biographical information provided in a candidate's curriculum vitae (CV) or resume for selection. This works on the principle that a "faculty-based view of a person's life" may be a good predictor of his job performance. Biodata contains such information as sex, age, family circumstances, education, professional qualification, previous employment history, and work experience, the position of responsibility outside work, leisure, interests, and career.

Biodata analysis is useful for screening job applicants who clearly do not meet the minimum requirements for the job. However, as a predictor of performance, this tool cannot be regarded as possessing much reliability. CVs in today's world are often cooked up by job applicants. It is not a transparent method as it has elements of bias. It is viewed as outdated due to the limitations it has in capturing applicants' abilities and potential holistically.

Work Samples and Simulations:

They are situations (techniques) that duplicate, as

nearly as possible, the actual conditions encountered on a job. It is a carefully developed exercise, modeled on realistic situations, in which the candidate participates and receives feedback. They are useful for jobs in which the cost and risk of mistakes are high, for example, in the training of pilots. The methods that fall under this heading are discussed below:

Role Play:

This is just like acting out a given role as in a stage play. Each job candidate takes the role of a person affected by an issue and studies the impacts of the issues on human life and/or the effects of human activities on the world around us from the perspective of that person. Role-playing is used in determining interpersonal skills, such as managerial and sales activities. As drama, the applicant adopts a relevant role, e.g., manager, salesperson, customer, debtor, creditor, etc., and plays it out. In this case, the job seeker wears someone else's shoes for the purpose of determining the physio-social characteristics of the person and situation. Role-playing, the approach, is a learning method developed from social learning theory. The candidates are required to enact defined roles based on an oral or written description of a situation. The steps involved in role-playing include defining objectives, choosing context and roles, introducing the exercise, role-play, concluding the discussion, and assessment. Types of role-playing may be multiple role-plays, single role-play, role rotation, and spontaneous role play.

Case studies:

These are actual events or situations of organizational problems, which are written descriptions for discussion purposes. It is also a real-life or hypothetical story or incident, and a set of questions that follow. The candidates are asked to analyze the event or circumstances with the objective of identifying the problems, tracing the cause of it, and finding solutions to it. A case study allows the application of theoretical concepts to be demonstrated, thus bridging the gap between theory and practice, encourages active participation, and provides an opportunity for determining key skills such as communication, group work, and problem-solving. This method is suitable for selecting the top and senior managers.

Management Games:

This is also known as business games. It is devised on the model of a business situation. For example, candidates may be divided into groups representing the management of competing firms. They make decisions like in real-life situations. This method is used in ascertaining candidates with skills for practical assessment of priorities and decision-making, analytical, logical, and reasoning capabilities, teamwork, time management, and leadership capabilities. The use of management games can help identify candidates who have innovative mechanisms for coping with stress.

In-Basket Exercise:

This is also known as the In-Tray method. Several memos are put into a tray, and candidates are expected to make sense out of them. The documents contain business problems that the candidate is to decide upon. The document may include e-mail, SMSs, reports, memos, and other items. Now the applicant is asked to prioritize the decisions to be made immediately and the ones that can be delayed.

Background Checks:

This is verification of the job seeker's employment history, education, credit history, drug screening, and criminal records, to ascertain his/her suitability for the job. Pre- employment background checks provide valuable insight when considering whether a candidate matches the job or not, and tend to enhance the credibility and trustworthiness of prospective candidates.

Background checks are used to verify information submitted by candidates-those relating to former employers, personal references, learning institutions, and other relevant agencies. It is the duty of employers to take extra care in ensuring that their employees are safe when a new member of staff comes into an organization. Most importantly, it improves the quality of hire by ensuring that vacant positions are filled with those who meet set criteria, including good past records. Background checks can help identify potential red flags, as well as mitigate the chances of hiring people with problematic backgrounds or behavior that may pose a risk to the organization. For example, if someone is convicted of theft or embezzlement of funds, he/she may not be suitable for managing the finances of a company. Similarly, if one has a drunk driving offence, he/she may not be employed as a driver for the company. These decisions may go a long way in reducing legal and financial risk for business concerns. Through background checks, the company's reputation and assets may be safeguarded, thereby enhancing its ethical standards. If a company's reputation is tarnished, this may result in a lack of trust by relevant stakeholders and may affect the bottom line negatively. In addition, pre-employment background checks may also be a way of adhering to legal and industry standards in many countries. However, we offer some tips: it is advisable to seek the permission of the job candidate before embarking on background checks. Any investigation should be job-related and demonstrate a clear connection with the job requirements. It should be the same for all candidates who applied for the job.

Reference Checks/Letters Recommendations:

This involves verifying information given by applicants and obtaining additional feedback on applications. The candidate is asked to supply two or three names of referees, previous employers, schoolteachers, neighbors, and friends as references. The purpose of a reference is to obtain confidential information about prospective employees. The information is further used to ascertain his/her character and suitability for the job. It is another step in the selection process. Speaking with individuals who have worked with a candidate in the past can be a good source of ascertaining his/her work performance and behavior, strengths and weaknesses, and overall suitability for the vacant position. By extension, reference checks can help verify the accuracy of information supplied by job applicants, increase confidence in the hiring process, and ensure a good match between candidates and their roles.

However, reference checks and letters of recommendation have fared badly as a means of selecting job candidates. Employers and individuals who make references or recommendations tend to avoid highly detrimental remarks either out of charity or because they think anything they say may be construed as slanderous or libelous. In some circumstances, references from individuals are entirely useless as they tend to speak in favor of the job applicant while concealing his/her negative character. This is probably because nobody will use their enemy as a referee. To solve the above problem, we recommend telephone references be used as an alternative or in addition to written references. This is because people are likely to give an honest opinion orally rather than commit the same in writing. This will certainly save time when decisions need to be made very fast.

Social Media Screening:

A job applicant's social media profiles offer insight into their personality, professionalism, qualifications and skills, cultural fitness, creativity, and innovation. The popularity of social media screening has grown with the advent of information technology and especially with platforms like Twitter, Facebook, X, TikTok, and LinkedIn. SHRM (2016) surveys show that 84% of companies use social media for recruitment, and 43% for job seekers. A similar survey by Ranosa (2019) indicates that 70% of HR professionals and managers use social media to get more information about job applicants. With social media, recruiters can gain a holistic view of applicants with respect to their personality, interests, and values that may not be discernible from a resume, cover letter, or interview. Hence, the information gathered by recruiters via social media can go a long way to determine whether a candidate would be hired or not (Ranosa, 2019). It is cost-friendly, while background checks are available at a fee, social media screening comes with little or no cost (Jeske & Shultz, 2015).

Test Methods:

A good test method is one that provides valid data that enables reliable prediction of behavior to be made, and therefore assists in the process of making an objective and reasoned decision when selecting people for jobs. With the help of test methods, organizations identify job applicants' capabilities and how they can adapt to their job environments. Using a test (or any selection tool) assumes the tool is both valid and reliable. Reliability is the first requirement of a test. A reliable test or selection tool is one that yields consistent scores when a person takes two alternate forms of the test or when he takes the same test on two or more different occasions. There are many ways of determining the reliability or consistency of a selection tool.

First, you can administer the same test to the same people at two different points in time and then compare the test scores. This is referred to as a retest estimate. Secondly, an internal comparison estimate can be applied. A test's internal consistency is a reliability measure. This is one reason why we find repetitive questions on some test questionnaires.

While reliability answers the question of how consistently a test measures whatever it is designed to measure, it does not prove that you are measuring what you intend to measure. On the other hand, validity tells you whether the test is measuring what you think it is supposed to measure. It is the correctness of the inferences that we can make based on the test. With the employee selection test, validity often refers to the evidence that the test is job related. This is to say that performance on the test is a valid predictor of subsequent performance on the job.

The validity of a test can be determined using test validity. It answers the question of whether the test measures what it is supposed to measure. For example, if Mrs. Abu gets a higher score on the secretarial skills test than Mrs. Obi, this presupposes that Mrs. Abu will do better on secretarial duties. There are two major ways of demonstrating test validity: criterion validity and content validity.

The content validity shows that the test constitutes a fair sample of the job's content. The job tasks that are critical to performance must be identified, and the task to be tested must be randomly selected as a sample of those tasks to test. If the task is chosen as a representative sample of what the person needs to know for the job, then the test is more likely to be content-valid. Criterion validity is a measurement or test score that relates to the criterion (i.e., performance on the job). Demonstrating criterion validity means that those who do well on thetest will also do well on the job and vice versa. Test scores are useful in selecting employees, and some of the tests are discussed below:

Personality Tests:

Personality tests are a set of unique characteristics that define an individual and differentiate them from others. These characteristics may include traits, behaviors, and patterns, extroversion or introversion, openness, agreeableness, and neuroticism, which may affect the way we think, feel, and interact with things around us. It is used in the employee selection process as a supplement to traditional interviews to match candidates to job roles and also to assess their cultural fitness, with the ultimate aim of improving retention as well as job performance. According to Techneeds (2025), over 70% of companies use personality tests to predict how candidates will perform in specific roles and integrate with group dynamics, so that not only competent people are selected, but also individuals who are compatible with the company's values and work environment. Many benefits are derived from the use of personality tests because they correlate with improved performance, reduced turnover, a more cohesive workplace culture, and higher job satisfaction. However, human resource practitioners should be mindful of the ethical implications of adopting personality assessment, especially as it concerns bias, privacy, and equity. In this regard, evaluations used should be both valid and reliable, thereby minimizing the risk of discrimination based on gender, ethnicity, or other protected characteristics. It is appropriate to use as a supplemental tool in the process of recruitment without ignoring the broader context of candidates' experiences and qualifications.

Situational Tests:

This is designed to measure how candidates respond and behave in hypothetical, job-related scenarios. It provides insight into how candidates might respond to challenges that may occur in real-life situations. The assessment may cover several issues that are important to an organization, such as conflict resolution, negotiation, ethics, decision-making, problem-solving, emotional intelligence, leadership, stress management, interpersonal skills, and teamwork, among others. For example, the test may evaluate a candidate's ability to make appropriate decisions in a work environment by mirroring the situation the candidate may encounter in the role he/she applied for. Those who score high in empathy may be placed in customer service, while assessment for a sales position may evaluate candidates on their negotiation skills and ethics. Situational tests can go a long way to improving the hiring process by ensuring that candidates with the right competencies are identified.

Cognitive Tests:

This test measures candidates' mental abilities and skills necessary in doing a job well, such as logical, verbal, and numerical reasoning, critical thinking, and problem-solving, among others (Outtz, 2002). Sometimes, cognitive tests can be mistaken for job-specific skills or an aptitude test. It must be mentioned that it does not measure personality characteristics like assertiveness, resilience, and creativity; the ability to control emotions and physical abilities. The core concept underlying an intelligence test is a measure of mental age. Mental age is generally indexed in terms of intelligence quotient (IQ) and calculated thus:

IQ = Mental Age Actual Age:

This means that the intelligence quotient is a ratio of

mental age, multiplied by 100. It is pertinent to mention that the intelligence quotient level varies because of culture and exposure. Intelligence testing assumes that if the organization can get bright and alert employees, quick at learning, it can train them faster than those who are less well- endowed. Intelligence tests have come to stay because of the belief that they correlate positively with performance (Outtz, 2002). Candidates selected on account of high intelligence quotient bring a contribution to their organization because:

- Logical reasoning skills will help employees make quality decisions, analyze situations, spot patterns, and solve complicated problems. Their critical thinking is an asset for research and the interpretation of research findings.
- Their verbal reasoning skills will enable them to understand and analyze written documents and draw logical conclusions. This skill is important in certain professions like human resource management, law, journalism, etc.
- Numerical skills are highly needed in some roles like accountancy, market research, HR analytics, and data presentation, amongst others.
- Due to their skills in problem-solving, they can identify problems and generate practical solutions.
- The ability to remember and recall information is important for business success and will help the organization in its learning and development activities.

Ability Tests:

An ability test is a means of measuring an individual's capacity in specific areas, under standardized conditions that allow the testers or administrators to make direct comparisons between individuals. They measure the ability for verbal reasoning, numerical reasoning, and general reasoning. These tests are further subdivided into aptitude tests, achievement tests, intelligence tests, and judgment tests.

Aptitude Tests:

This measures the ability and skill of candidates. It measures how well a prospective employee would be able to perform after training. It is used to predict future abilities and performance. One of the objectives is to advise job seekers regarding the fields of activity in which they are likely to succeed (vocational guidance). Other aptitude tests designed to measure special abilities include a mechanical aptitude test, a clerical aptitude test, an artistic aptitude test, a musical aptitude test, a management aptitude test, etc.

Achievement Tests:

These measure a person's potential in each activity, based on their skills and knowledge already acquired. Achievement tests can be used to offer admission to academic institutions. The grades in previous examinations are often used as indicators of achievement and potential for learning. This resembles the aptitude test, but the difference lies in the usage of results based on past achievements and performance. This can be illustrated thus: When you examine (test) the subject "mathematics," the result is his "achievement." But if you test a student to see whether he has the potential to embark on a certain career that is "aptitude." Suffice it to say that there is a thin line between aptitude and achievement tests.

Achievement tests can be called other names, like proficiency tests, performance tests, occupational, or trade tests.

Graphology:

This has to do with the analysis of handwriting. As a selection tool, it is widely used in France. But the origin of graphology is traced back to the eleventh century, when the Chinese drew attention to the relationship between handwriting and personality. With the use of graphology, a lot can be revealed about prospective candidates' degree of energy, inhibitions, leadership qualities, domination potentials, idiosyncrasies, and elements of balance and control, from which many personality characteristics can be inferred. The validity of handwriting analysis is not foolproof; some organizations use graphology tests to supplement other selection procedures. The major claims by the users of graphology are that it indicates stability over time and also shows consistency. On the flip side, candidates can distort their handwriting, resulting in faulty prediction with regard to job performance.

Polygraph Tests:

They are designed to confirm the accuracy of the information given on the application form. Polygraph is a lying dictator and helps organizations that are vulnerable to theft or swindling. A polygraph uses an electronic device for detecting lies from job candidates. Some electronic devices are wired on candidates, often without their knowledge or consent. This could be connected to a visual display in another room and used to monitor the candidate's heartbeat, body temperature, pulse rate, and other physiological details.

How to Validate a Test:

It is the duty of an industrial psychologist to conduct a validation study. But Human Resource Managers and any other person using tests or test results should know something about validation. Therefore, the steps involved in test validation include:

- Analyze the job: The first approach to test validation is to analyze the job and write job descriptions and job specifications. It is the human traits and skills that are required that will predict success on the job (predictors). At this first step, you must define what constitutes "success on the job" by using certain criteria, such as production-related criteria like quality, quantity, design, level of errors, speed of production, amongst others, and Personnel data such as absenteeism, commitment, loyalty, length of service, etc.

- Choose the test: Once you know the predictors, such as aggressiveness, extroversion, numerical ability, and technical skills, a test can be designed to test them. Usually, several tests are combined into a battery of tests. This is aimed at measuring an array of possible predictors.

- Administer the test: The test can be administered to current employees on the job, and then you can compare their test scores with their current performance. This is referred to as "concurrent validation." It has its own disadvantage in the sense that employees may not be a good representative of new applicants. The current employees have already had on-the-job training. The second approach is to administer tests to the applicants before you hire them. This is called "predictive validation." After hiring new applicants using only existing selection techniques (not the result of the new tests). Then, after they have been on the job, an analysis is carried out to see if there is a relationship between their performance and their earlier test scores. You can now determine whether you could have used their performance on the new test to predict their subsequent performance on the job.

- Relate your test scores and criteria: The next approach is to determine if there is a significant relationship between scores (predictor) and performance (criterion). The statistical relationship between scores on the test and performance, using correlation analysis, needs to be established, and the degree of statistical relationship noted.

- Cross-validate and revalidate: This requires one to perform the steps mentioned in items (c) and (d) above. Another way of handling this is to have someone revalidate the test periodically.

Advantages of Testing Methods:

- The benefits derived from the use of the test method in employee selection are as follows:
- Prediction of future performance: It can be used for hiring people, transfer, and promotion, all in the bid to improve performance in the future.
- Diagnoses of situation and behavior: A well-planned test helps to understand the situation and cause of the behavior. For example, the cause of absenteeism could be due to many factors, and tests can help us understand the cause of the human side.
- Offers the benefit of economies of scale: The use of tests on large groups saves both time and money.
- The unveiling of hidden talent: It helps to uncover the qualifications and talents of candidates that cannot be detected by an application form and interviews.
- An unbiased tool: It serves as an unbiased tool in the selection process because of its reliability and validity norms.

The problem of Test Methods of Selection:

Many of the test methods of selection were developed in the Western World. The problems of tests are their inability to satisfy reliability, validity, cultural sensitivity, and fairness criteria when applied in developing or third-world countries. The problem of measurement accuracy is always there because measurement in social and management sciences is indirect. In personnel selection, these problems are even more dominant because inaccurate measurements will render any instrument valueless, as it may not measure what it purports to measure (Hunter & Hunter, 1984). Other limitations of test methods are as follows:

- They cannot stand alone; hence, they are used as supplements to other selection methods.
- They are better at predicting failure than success. They often predict candidates who cannot perform satisfactorily, instead of those who can perform satisfactorily.
- They are not precise measures of one's skills and traits, but samples of one's total characteristics. Therefore, the test with the highest score does not necessarily mean better choices for a job than those with lower scores.

Final Decisions in Selection:

When the applicants have passed through the selection hurdle, and decisions are to be made on candidates to whom letters of appointment should be extended, it is important that the selection criteria are set up before the vacancy is advertised. By this, we mean the person specification. The setting of measurable criteria is important in the selection process (Ogunsola et al, 2023). This is because it is based on the criteria that job applicants will be measured against. The selection criteria will not only make it credible but also help adopt the most appropriate selection procedure. Selection criteria are often concentrated on the person specification (covering a whole range of skills, experience, qualifications, education, motivation, interest, personal attributes, etc.). Three approaches can be used to determine selection criteria. They are organizational fit, team/functional fit, and job fit:

- Organizational Fit: This refers to the criteria organizations are looking for in their employees. Organizations may be expecting their employees to possess flexible, desirable attitudes needed for business success, and commitment to goals. In an expanding and innovative organization, it will be required for the employees to be more flexible and adaptable, rather than the ability to do the job for which they were recruited.
- Functional and Team Fit: Some organizations depend largely on teamwork and committees to carry out their activities. This will require appropriate interpersonal skills for all members of the team or committee. The same functional criteria may be important when new members are to join existing teams.
- Individual Job Criteria: We can arrive at individual job criteria by analyzing the task to be done and then presenting them in the form of a job description. Also, from the job description, we can determine the personal qualities, attributes, or competencies required to do the task. Hence, the individual job criteria are embedded in the job description and person specifications.
- Another approach is to look at the individual job criteria and develop a competency profile as a means of setting

criteria against which to select. The competency profile should consist of personal skills, knowledge, motives, trials, etc., that are necessary for superior performance.

Job Offer:

One of the last elements in the process of selection is the offer of appointment letters. When this is received, an acceptance letter is usually expected from the candidate. The appointment letter contains the terms and conditions of the job, when and to whom the candidate should report, and those on the assumption of duty. It is, however, important that the selection process be seen as objective and fair to all job seekers so that those who may be rejected can attest that there is a level playing field for all participants and, above all, have a good impression of the organization. It is necessary for companies to maintain their reputation as decent employers. In fact, the final stage of the selection process is marked with physical and medical tests, satisfactory references, and an offer of employment letter.

After the job offer, the candidate may sign a written contract that specifies in more detail what is expected from the employee as well as the employer. This contract will be binding on both parties and will govern their relationship. A formal employment contract may cover issues around job security, duty of care, recognition, work-life balance, communication channels, opportunities for delegation and empowerment, etc. Apart from the written contract, there are other expectations of the employer and the employee that remain largely unwritten and yet influential in the future relationship of both parties. The term used to capture the unwritten contract is called the psychological contract.

Physical and Medical Examinations:

A physical and medical examination is conducted on the candidates who have passed the other preliminary hurdles. Certain jobs require physical qualities such as clear vision, acute hearing, and stamina, a clear tone of voice, and tolerance of arduous working conditions. This is necessary to determine the applicant's state of health and physical capability for the job. It is simple to detect whether the job applicant is carrying any infectious disease, to identify defects of an individual for undertaking such work that may be detrimental to their health. It protects the organization from paying compensation claims for injuries and accidents caused by pre-existing ailments.

Environmental Circumstances Influencing Selection:

There are many factors that can influence selection within the environment where the exercise is taking place. They are:

- The environment of the organization: The nature of the organization carrying out the selection has a profound effect on the selection process. In Nigeria, Public sector selection in top positions is either on political patronage or merit. The patronage system provides jobs for those who worked to elect politicians. In the private sector, it is mainly done on merit and to some extent, based on friendship with managers or employees of the organization. Pure 'merit' (i.e., selection based only on an employee's excellence in abilities and experience) is indeed the most ideal, which strategic human resource management tries to achieve but seldom does. Other aspects of the organization that affect selection are the size, complexity, and technological volatility. It is costly to develop and use systematic, reliable, and valid personnel selection tools, so only large organizations can afford to use the techniques, and the large organizations must be stable in both technology and jobs; otherwise, it will not be cost-effective.

- Nature of the labor market: The next factor affecting the selection in organizations is the labor market, with which the organization must deal. The labor market of the organization is affected by the labor market of the country. For example, the Nigerian labor market is currently saturated with lots of unemployed men and women, among whom, only a few have the requisite knowledge and skills. The reason is that we, people who graduated ten to twenty years ago, had never worked in structured organizations and had little or no job experience. Nobody can buy experience; it is gained through consistent practice and continuous learning. The environmental circumstances affecting selection are further influenced by the working conditions organizations offer, the job itself, and the organization's image.

- Union requirements: In some organizations where the

union is powerful and has succeeded in extracting some kind of contract from the organization, selection would be based on seniority (experience on the job with the organization) as a major criterion; this will certainly affect the organization's selection process.

- Government regulations: In government organizations in Nigeria, selection complies with the rule on 'Federal Character,' which specifies how the selection is to be done in public organizations. Also, many Western countries prohibit employers from asking prospective employees questions about their race, sex, age, and so on. Even indirect questions, to some extent, are not allowed.

Why Careful Recruitment/Selection Is Important:

Carefully planned and executed selection of the process is important for three reasons:

- Performance: The performance of any organization depends on its employees. However, these are employees who have been carefully selected and who possess the right skills. It will affect performance adversely if the wrong people are employed owing to the faulty selection process.
- Cost: Organizations that have good selection processes can always reduce the cost of doing business; if not in the short run, this can be seen in the long run. When employees with the right capabilities are selected and properly placed, they will be more efficient and perform better than those who are misfits. However, if the wrong people are recruited, it could prove expensive for an

organization. Also, if they happen to exit too early after their selection, the whole process of recruitment/selection must be repeated, with the implication of additional cost and time, too.

- Legal obligations: The governments of many countries of the world are showing an increasing tendency to intervene in the labor market by passing legislation. Some legal implications may arise when the hiring process is not properly carried out. In the first instance, it may lead to negligent hiring. This means that the organizations have hired people with criminal records (i.e., criminals with questionable character), who may use their access to customers to commit crimes. In a matter where a company is negligent for not cross-checking properly, it may not absolve itself from liability. Secondly, selection processes had to be carried out in such a way that they do not involve defamation of character. Thirdly, any breach of the labor laws relating to recruitment/selection could result in an added cost in the form of fines and may have a bad reputation for treating people unfairly, which may impact negatively on the future of such an organization.
- Workforce diversity: It is obvious that the workforce is becoming heterogeneous; with globalization, more women are coming into the labor market. Also, aged individuals and people have access to the employment market. All this has put demands on HR professionals to be careful in recognizing workforce diversity, flextime, the aging population, and people's changing attitudes, without which the recruitment/selection may not achieve its intended purposes.

Legal and Ethical Issues in Employee Recruitment and Selection:

Recruitment and selection as a human resource process is a serious matter, in that if it is not properly handled, it can result in litigation. To avoid legal traps, human resources practitioners should ensure compliance with all relevant laws and regulations at the federal, state, and local levels. It behooves human resources managers and company attorneys to have an understanding of and be guarded by the laws of the countries where they operate their businesses. For example, in the United States, one must be aware of the US Equal Employment Opportunity Commission (EEOC). This is anti-discrimination legislation that does not allow employers to make employment decisions because of race, sex (including pregnancy), ethnicity, citizenship, age, color, national origin, sexual orientation, or genetic information. Instead, employment decisions, including recruitment and selection, work assignment, progressive discipline, promotion, and compensation, must be job-related and consistent with business necessity. Other acts under the Equal Employment Opportunity that should be of interest to HR practitioners in the US are the Americans with Disabilities Act (ADA), which prohibits discrimination against qualified individuals due to their disability; the Genetic Nondiscrimination Act (GINA), which prohibits discrimination against individuals based on their genetic information when making employment decisions;

Pregnancy Discrimination Act, among others.

HR professionals must basically avoid two types of discrimination– namely, disparate treatment and disparate impact. Disparate treatment occurs when applicants are treated differently on account of their membership in a protected class (national origin, sex, or race). Whereas disparate impact is usually unintended and results from policies that appear to be neutral but have a discriminatory effect. It occurs when the selection rate for an employment decision works to the disadvantage of a protected class. This becomes glaring when the selection rate of a protected class is less than 80% of the class with the highest selection rate. For this reason, employers of labor must ensure that selection or recruitment tools do not have disparate treatment or disparate impact. Therefore, the following recruitment and selection processes need to be carried out diligently:

- Job Advertisement: When planning to do a job posting, attention should be paid to the wording before placing it in a newspaper or job portal. The job posting must not contain any information that gives preference to a person's race, religion, gender, or age. Disability, color, and sexual orientation. The US Equal Employment Commission considers it illegal to discriminate against any of these factors. Additionally, any selection instruments used to screen candidates must be properly validated to confirm they assess job– relevant criteria and neither discriminate against protected groups nor compromise applicant privacy.

- Interviews: Care must be exercised with regard to the kind of questions asked during an interview session, such that questions considered discriminatory are avoided. For example, it may not be proper to make it mandatory for candidates to indicate their age or gender. Also, you cannot ask a job candidate if she has children of school age or if she is pregnant. Similarly, in cases of disability, one of the requirements of EEOC is that the employer provides reasonable accommodation for the job applicant, except if the provision of this accommodation will create significant difficulty or where the cost is affordable. Identifying reasonable accommodation is an interactive process between the job applicant and the employer, but the applicant must request it or show he/she need it. The golden rule is not to ask candidates about their disability or to ask their former employer for a reference. The most important thing is to cross-check the laws of the respective states where the job is domiciled; for instance, it is illegal to deny a job candidate employment on account of their credit history, particularly in California, Maryland, Oregon, Washington, Hawaii, and Connecticut. Employers must demonstrate responsibility in conducting interviews and other associated functions, and do so within the confines of the law, in such a way that an individual's privacy is not violated. In this vein, overly invasive and discriminatory background checks must be avoided.
- Final Offer: A letter of employment is only issued to candidates who emerged successful in a fair and transparent recruitment and selection process. These are candidates who satisfied the selection criteria. After

issuing a letter conveying a job offer, the next activity is to sign a contract of employment. Most organizations couch this contract into an employee handbook or employee manual, which explains the company's systems and processes, including its values, guidelines, and polices. It sets expectations for the employee and the employer, which may result in the smooth running of the organization and, most importantly, make the company less vulnerable in terms of litigation since it provides clarity on a wide range of issues. For example, some employee manuals make policies on anti-discrimination, thereby complying with the latest federal, state, and local laws. Due to the multi-faceted nature of the employee handbook, it has become an effective tool for employee engagement and motivation, and a means of building a positive and productive workplace culture.

In view of the above, a company that wants to stay within the limit of the law should not reject candidates for reasons that are not relevant to the job. It is also important to standardize the recruitment and selection processes and apply them to all job candidates irrespective of their religion, age, gender, or demographic group, as it will help ensure fairness and transparency across all groups. Additionally, avoiding derogatory statements and language that connotes discrimination will save a company from legal actions, including proper pronouns like-he/she/they. Lastly, candidates should not be asked illegal questions, especially questions regarding marital status, intention to have children, or whether a candidate is pregnant or not.

Others include medical conditions, except that it was stated ab initio as relevant to the performance of the job, race, ethnicity, physical and mental health, and sexual orientation. The question varies from nation to nation.

References

Armstrong, M (2012). Armstrong's Handbook of Human Resource Practice, London, Kogan Page.

Cai, W. (2023). Formalizing the Informal: Adopting a formal culture-fit measurement system in the employee-selection process. Account. Rev., 98(3), pp. 47–70.

Hunter J. E., Hunter R. F. (1984). Validity and utility of alternate predictors of job performance. Psychol. Bull. 96, 72–98. 10.1037/0033-2909.96.1.72 [DOI] [Google Scholar]

Hermelin et al. (2007). The Validity of Assessment Centers for the Prediction of Supervisory Performance Ratings. International Journal of Selection and Assessment 15(4):405-411. DOI:10.1111/j.1468 2389.2007. 00399. X.

Jeske, D., & Shultz, K. S. (2015). Using social media content for screening in recruitment and selection: pros and cons. Work, Employment and Society, 30(3), 535–546.

https://doi.org/10.1177/0950017015613746

Kapur, R. (2018). Recruitment and selection.

International Journal of Advancement in Social Science and Humanity, 5(1), 1–13.

https://sdbindex.com/documents/00000474/00001-48043.pdf

Kaushik, A. (2025). 18 Effective employee selection methods in 2025.

https://www.wecreateproblems.com/blog/employee-selection-methods

Kleinmann, M. and Ingold, P. V. (2019). Toward a better understanding of assessment centers: A conceptual review. Annual Review of Organizational Psychology and Organizational Behavior. 6:349 372.

https://doi.org/10.1146/annurev-orgpsych-012218-014955

Ogunsola, et al (2023). Employee selection process: An approach for effective organizational performance.

International Journal of Social Science and Human Research, 6(10), 6132-614. DOI: https://doi.org/10.47191/ijsshr/v6-i10-47

Outtz, J. (2002). The role of cognitive ability tests in employment selection. Human Performance 15(1), 161-171.

DOI: 10.1207/S15327043HUP1501&02_10

Pshdar Abdalla Hamza et al. (2021). Recruitment and Selection: The Relationship between Recruitment and Selection with Organizational Performance. International Journal of Engineering, Business and Management (IJEBM). 5(3), DOI: https://dx.doi.org/10.22161/ijebm.5.3

Ranosa, R. (2019). How recruiters check for red flags on social media. https://www.hcamag.com/us/specialization/hr-technology/how-recruiters-check-for-red-flags-on- social-media/189898

Schmidt, F. L. and Hunter, J. E. (1998). The validity and utility of selection methods in personnel psychology: Practical and theoretical implications of 85 years of research findings. Psychological Bulletin, 124 (2), 262–274.

SHRM (2016) Survey: Employers are using social media to find passive candidates.

https://www.shrm.org/topics-tools/news/talent-acquisition/survey-employers-using-social-media-to-find-passive-candidates

Tech needs (2025). The role of human resource personality tests in effective hiring.

https:www.techneeds.com/2025/03/21/the-role-of-human-resource-personality-tests-in-effective-hiring/

Towers Perrin (2003). Working Today: Understanding What Drives Employee Engagement.

Towers Perrin Talent Report. Retrieved from.

https://studylib.net/doc/12886509/understanding-

what-drives-employee-engagement-working-

tod.

Chapter Four: Employee Onboarding and Socialization

Introduction.

It takes employers a lot of time, money, and effort to hire an individual employee. Even when the right candidate has been chosen, it should not be taken for granted that the new entrant knows everything. He/she is new to the job responsibilities, the company philosophy, culture, health, safety policies, and even where the restrooms are located. The process of onboarding and socialization integrates newcomers into their company's vision and mission, as well as the role they are expected to play. Starting a job for a newcomer can be a challenging experience as it involves learning the way the organization functions, its cultures, and values. Adapting to an unknown environment with the complexities of the modern workplace may not be like a walk in the park, hence the need for organizations to make a conscious effort in helping employees settle down quickly in the discharge of their roles and responsibilities. Many organizations have specific actions and/or practices they apply to facilitate the introduction of new employees to the structure and culture of their work environment. Some terms like employee socialization, onboarding, orientation, and induction are often used interchangeably to describe how new employees are integrated into an organization, adjusting to their roles and responsibilities; to improve retention, engagement, and productivity; understand company culture, expectations, and policies; and reduce uncertainty and anxiety. These terms, though they may be similar, have distinct meanings, and their differences are significant, impacting employee experiences. The focus area, duration, key activities, and scope of these terminologies are presented below:

Table 4.1:

Term	Focus Area	Duration	Key Activities	Scope
Orientation	Immediate logistics, policies & basic setup	1–3 days	Tour, paperwork, HR policies, introductions, formal and procedural	Narrow (surface-level)
Induction	Formal welcome, values & structures	1–2 weeks	Official welcome, job-specific training, team integration, semi-formal	Medium (Moderate)
Onboarding	Full integration, role clarity, performance & tools	Weeks to months	Role training, mentoring, performance goals, feedback loops, strategic, and role-specific	Broad & deepening
Socialization	Cultural assimilation, culture, norms & informal networks	Ongoing	Learning norms, values, and informal networks, adapting behavior, informal, experimental	Deep & long-term

Definition of terms.

Employee Orientation:

Orientation is a subset of onboarding, whereby new

employees are introduced to their role, team, and overall organizational culture. It is a process of introducing new hires to the company's mission, culture, and structure while outlining their role and expectations (Gibbons, 2025; Villanueva, 2025). This is perhaps the initial stage of the onboarding process that helps employees have basic knowledge of the company's mission, vision, values, policies, and procedures, including where the bathrooms are and how to log into the email. The aim is to familiarize new employees with the work environment, help them complete essential new hire paperwork, answer questions that may help them assume their new position, and provide opportunities to meet people, socialize, and start building relationships. Though orientation, depending on the company and the role the new employee is to play, can take a few hours or days, it is narrow in scope and contributes to the overall onboarding experience.

Employee Induction:

This is a broader and more formalized version of orientation, often used in structured organizations to officially welcome new employees, give them job-specific training, and integrate them into their team or units. It includes ceremonial welcomes and deeper introductions to the company's mission and values. Armstrong (2006) defines induction as the process of receiving and welcoming employees when they first join organizations and giving them the basic information, they need to settle down quickly and happily, to start work. The author outlines four (4) primary aims of induction: (1) to smoothen the career journey of new employees, at the onset when everything appears strange and unfamiliar; (2) creating favorable impression of the company in the mind of the new employee, to elicit their loyalty; (3) to induct new employees to a culture of high performance in the shortest possible time; and (4) to reduce turnover rate and improve employee retention. Employee induction is like orientation because the focus is to acquaint new members of staff with the company's goals and objectives, and the role they have been hired to perform, and make them valuable members of the team. Newcomers should be clear about what is expected in terms of work and behavior. The concept of induction is to introduce new entrants into an existing group of people, in an organization, and help them have a sense of belonging (Morris, 2021; Sarpita, 2022). What to include in an induction program varies from company to company. It may comprise receiving employees when they begin work; tours of offices, factories, and facilities; introducing them to the company and their colleagues; and informing them of the activities, customs, and traditions of the company (Salau et al., 2014).

Employee Onboarding:

Unlike orientation or induction, employee onboarding is a comprehensive and strategic process, providing a more extended and immersive experience, involving the integration of the employee into the company culture and their continuous development within the organization. It is like orientation and induction because it aims at connecting the employee to his/her job. According to Bhadane et al (2025), onboarding is a set of integration programs that provide new employees with the necessary resources to become fully engaged and culturally aware members of a productive workforce. It commences from the moment a job candidate accepts his/her offer of employment to when the employee is fully acclimatized with the company, which can take as long as one year. Onboarding can be considered as not only full integration into one's job role but also into the company's culture, the long-term career path, and the development of meaningful relationships within the organization. Today, onboarding has become an organizational strategy in the acquisition of essential knowledge, skills, and behaviors required for adaptation to the new workplace because of the significant learning and development processes involved. Some researchers see it as a crucial transition or a new job for candidates from outsiders to insiders within the organization to enable employees to become productive as quickly as possible. Unlike orientation or induction, which are necessary for logistical and basic understanding of organizational processes, onboarding goes the extra mile in building strong relationships, employee engagement, loyalty, and long-term job satisfaction. This represents a shift from a transactional to a relational approach of managing human capital, to equipping the employees with the tools, knowledge, and relationships they need to succeed in their roles. (Kuursisto, 2024 & Reesse, 2025).

Brief history of onboarding:

The term-onboarding is the newest terminology describing employees' integration and socialization in organizational settings. It was coined in the United States of America in the 1970s as a management jargon, encompassing more intentional efforts on the part of the organization to help employees acclimate to their roles, teams, and organizational culture. Though at this period, onboarding was limited in scope and duration. However, by the 1990s, the concept of onboarding had evolved into a formalized process that could span weeks and months, representing a paradigm shift from similar terms like orientation and induction, to recognizing that early employee experiences could influence long-term performance and satisfaction. This is perhaps the foundation of the strategic approach in the onboarding process, whereby organizations introduce training modules, mentorship programs, and performance check-ins, feedback, and evaluations. The focus of the onboarding process is to create a long- term relationship between the new hire and the employer over the employee's duration of employment.

Between 2010 and to date, academic models on onboarding have emerged, such as those propounded by Bauer & Erdogan (2011), which describe the onboarding phases (pre-arrival, encounter, and adjustment), including behavioral anchors and how to align onboarding to organizational goals. This framework has been helpful to

HR practitioners who want to transform newcomers from organizational outsiders into insiders, using each of the onboarding phases to support psychological adjustment, performance readiness, and cultural integration of new employees.

Today, the digital revolution has crept into onboarding processes, and organizations are adapting online portals, e-learning platforms, and automated workflows to streamline onboarding. This is with the aim of reducing administrative costs and making skills and knowledge available across locations, departments, and job levels. During the COVID-19 pandemic and the consequent lockdown of workplaces, digital onboarding became more prominent, prompting organizations to rethink how they build connection and culture virtually. This trend has remained a significant feature of onboarding in many organizations. To achieve long-term success, onboarding is becoming increasingly personalized, data-driven, and continuous; integrating elements of DEI (diversity, equity, and inclusion), PMS (performance management systems), mental health, and career pathing, etc.

Employee Socialization:

This is a long-term process of how employees internalize the company culture, build relationships, and learn how things really work beyond the handbook. According to Sakes (2018), organizational socialization is the process through which a new member of an organization learns the required attitudes and behaviors that are necessary to be an effective member of an organization. Another definition has it as strategic human resource management tools that help employees connect to the new working environment through their head and heart (Subedi and Karkee, 2020). Yet fathers of organizational socialization view it "as the process by which an employee acquires social skills and knowledge necessary to assume an organizational role" (Maanen and Schein 1979: 211). The implications of all these definitions are that socialization is a long-term process aimed at assisting employees in understanding informal rules, behavioral expectations, and cultural nuances of their organization. New employees, as a matter of necessity, must acquire attitudes, behaviors, and knowledge needed to successfully participate as organizational members. As a process, it involves helping newcomers develop a sense of belonging; aligning their personal values with organizational objectives; providing an enabling environment to navigate informal networks and understand power structures; and assisting them to fit the social fabric of the business environment. While socialization is like other processes that help integrate new employees into an organization so that they can become valuable organizational members, socialization stands apart as a deeper, ongoing process that shapes how employees internalize the culture, norms, and values of their workplace.

Employee socialization could be the process by which

new employees understand the company's policies, the internal culture, how the company hierarchy works, and the ways to function effectively in the organization. Developing programs and policies that integrate new employees into the company helps the company maintain a consistent corporate culture. A new employee is like a raw material that awaits organizational molding or socialization to become fully operational as a member of the group. New employees come into an organization with considerable potential that needs to be translated into actual and meaningful output. The workplace is a network of relationships among individuals, of which social interaction is essential. To achieve this objective, the individual must be socialized in the culture of the organization he/they gained employment. Socialization transforms newcomers into productive and accepted members of an organization. While this applies to new employees, it can also apply to transferred and promoted employees within an organization; when they begin to acquaint themselves with the goals and values of their jobs, the challenges of their new roles, and establish themselves as well as make themselves accepted members of the group they are working with.

The general assumption is that people who are well socialized into an organization are more likely to stay and develop their careers with that organization. This is a critical process for individuals pursuing successful careers and for organizations building effective workforces.

Building a competent workforce, one where people believe they fit in well with their organizations, is often viewed as a competitive edge in today's business. For organizations, a competent and committed workforce minimizes costly turnover and selection expenses. Moreover, individual employee attributes associated with successful organizational socialization can accumulate across the organization to positively affect organizational performance and effectiveness.

The organizational socialization process is complex because it involves actions taken by both the newcomer and the organization, and lessons learned may be intentional or unintentional. Newcomers will go through a socialization process, regardless of what the organization may or may not do; thus, good human resource management would prescribe some planning to guide employee adjustment to the job and organization. Transparent human resource practices that support the organization's mission and values are more likely to help employees make sense of their roles in the organization than management practices that conflict with or confuse employees. The mix of formal organizational interventions (e.g., Training) and informal interventions (e.g., a mentor) may not provide compatible lessons. For example, mentors can provide an informal, personal socialization process when senior members tutor junior members and groom them for successful careers within the organization. Although this mentoring may be informal, managers and supervisors who are likely to be mentors can be formally trained to provide positive socialization experiences for their newcomers. Company manuals can help newcomers learn important acronyms and jargon that distinguish organizational members. Employee handbooks can shape newcomer expectations and identify the behaviors and customs of insiders that the organization would like to promote. New employees should adhere to the organization's dress code and be sensitive to behaviors that are judged to be acceptable or unacceptable by management, including learning jargon and acronyms that identify them as insiders.

Employee socialization not only helps new employees understand corporate culture, but it also encourages the development of teamwork between new employees and current staff members. Allowing employees to become more familiar on a social as well as a professional level can develop strong bonds that improve productivity and help to reduce employee turnover. For individuals, a good fit within the organization can lead to several positive benefits. People who are well socialized are more committed to their organizations, more satisfied with their jobs, and earn more than people who do not learn to fit in with their organizations. Furthermore, people who are well socialized are less likely to quit their jobs and more likely to build successful careers within the organization. The extent to which both organizational and individual socialization processes support a good person-organization fit will define the extent to which that individual has been successfully socialized. Having defined our terms, the rest of this chapter will concentrate on onboarding and socialization processes since they have stronger and long-term effects on employee retention, productivity, and satisfaction.

The purpose of employee onboarding:

Onboarding is the bridge between recruiting the right people and enabling them to achieve peak performance. When new employees are recruited, the process of fully integrating and acclimatizing them with their new company is called onboarding, so that they are equipped with the tools they need and embedded into the culture and rhythm of the organization. The purpose of a successful onboarding program is to connect new employees to the company's goals and objectives and thus prepare the ground for employee engagement and loyalty. The purpose of employee onboarding is discussed below:

Clarity rather than guesswork:

Onboarding helps new employees have an understanding of what their roles and responsibilities are, thereby eliminating ambiguity and confusion. Good onboarding not only ensures that expectations are comprehended but also that the new employees have the necessary skills and abilities to contribute to organizational success. Hence, onboarding programs should be replete with clear communications centered around expectations and how new employees can fit in the big picture, and the kind of behaviors that are encouraged and discouraged within a particular organizational culture.

Connection employees to culture:

Onboarding familiarizes new employees with the new organization, including co-workers, and helps them assimilate into the company's culture, vision, mission, and core values. It has the propensity to build relationships with managers, teammates, mentors, and cross-functional partners, and early cultural fitness. The truth is that human beings are wired for connection, of which onboarding provides opportunities for. These early connections are necessary to understand decision-making patterns, team dynamics, and particularly how employees collaborate, communicate, and contribute. When new employees immerse organizational norms (unwritten, and mutually agreeable rules), they become organizational members (insiders) rather than outsiders. It helps employees feel seen, valued, and part of something bigger.

Early engagement and growth:

Onboarding showcases a lot of opportunities in the areas of career paths, learning resources, and internal mobility that may be of interest to new employees, and employees who see a future within the organization are more likely to stay. Onboarding should offer structured pathways for integrating new employees, providing feedback, mentoring, and early wins, which keep motivation levels high. Investment in onboarding pays off because it lays the foundation for long-term employee engagement and trust.

Retention and performance:

It is not enough to just hire new employees; the main job is in keeping them, and this is where onboarding comes in. Onboarding is the strategic process that integrates people into their company and job responsibilities, as well as setting the tone for an employee's entire journey. Research has consistently shown that onboarding leads to employee retention and high performance (Didion et al, 2024). For example, when employees feel connected to the team and aligned with company values, they derive a sense of belonging, which is a key driver of retention. They would also be more invested in their work, going the extra mile, physically and emotionally connected to their responsibilities. Similarly, onboarding is a chance to reinforce goal setting and accountability, and by doing so, organizations create a culture of high performance. When companies treat onboarding as a strategic priority, they empower their employees and improve performance metrics.

Onboarding Processes:

Effective organizations devote time and resources to creating onboarding programs and apply different approaches to realizing it, but no matter what the approach may consist of, the major goal is to integrate the newcomer into the organizational system and make him/her feel welcomed and prepared for the responsibilities ahead. This is necessary because every organizational member needs to have a shared vision and understand how they can successfully contribute to the company's mandate. Basically, new entrants are introduced to their responsibilities and the teams they are to work with because collaboration is vital. Also, they are educated about the company's goals, values, policies, and procedures, and how to imbibe the culture of the organization (Bell, 2021 Organizations classify their onboarding programs into formal and informal.

. The formal onboarding is properly structured and planned programs designed to integrate newcomers into their roles, teams, and organizational processes (Frögéli et al, 2023). Depending on how it is crafted, it may include orientation/induction sessions; training modules, performance expectations and measurement standards; compliance and policy briefings, etc. On the other hand, informal onboarding is organic, unstructured, without a specific plan, and is aimed at helping new hires learn the social norms, values, and unwritten rules of the workplace. The activities of informal onboarding are varied and may include casual meetings and conversations with colleagues, observing team dynamics, taking part in social events, mentorship, and informal feedback. Formal and informal onboarding are not competing, but complementary in the efforts to shape new entrants' experiences. While formal onboarding programs can last for days, weeks, or months, informal onboarding is ongoing and evolves naturally through interactions and experiences (Ogunbukola, 2024; Frögéli et al, 2023). There is a need to blend both approaches to grow a richer and more resilient workforce ready to thrive in today's complex work environments. While formal onboarding ensures consistency, accountability, and clarity across the organization, informal onboarding introduces newcomers to the social norms and values in building trust and relationships, cultural assimilation, informal power structures, and a sense of belongingness.

Table 4.2: Onboarding Process:

Aspect	Formal Onboarding	Informal Onboarding
Structure	Planned and scheduled	Spontaneous and organic
Duration	Defined (days to months)	Ongoing
Led by	HR, managers, trainers	Peers, mentors, team culture
Focus	Role clarity, compliance, performance	Social norms, relationships, culture
Measurement	Milestones, checklists, surveys	Observational, anecdotal

Onboarding process plays a vital role in shaping how new employees transition from outsiders to fully engaged contributors. It begins the moment a job offer is accepted and can extend over several weeks or months. Unlike orientation, which focuses on logistics and compliance, onboarding is about integration into the role, the team, and the company culture. This section outlines the key phases of the onboarding journey, from pre-onboarding to long-term engagement. Outlined below in depth are each of the key onboarding elements, showing how they work together to create a seamless and empowering experience for new employees:

Pre-boarding:

Onboarding process begins the moment the job candidate accepts his/her offer of appointment, before the new employee sets foot into the office, building anticipation and reducing uncertainty. Like behind-the-scenes preparation, it is good practice to send out emails and provide some basic information to employees about the first day by listing what to expect, to significantly ease their transition. Other logistics that should be available include videos from the team or leadership to create a warm first impression; digital forms for tax, benefits, and contracts sent ahead of time to streamline the first day; setting up laptops, software access, and email accounts; and sharing company handbooks and organization charts to familiarize new hires with the environment, with the view to creating excitement, reducing first-day anxiety and building early engagement. It is important to send an email to the new employee to answer questions like: what time and day the onboarding is starting; where to log in (in the virtual onboarding or where to go in the case of on-site onboarding; and a contact person if there are questions.

Welcome and Orientation:

Orientation is typically the first formal interaction between the new employee and the company. It is a day of warm introduction to the company's ethos and expectations, creating a sense of belonging and furnishing the crucial insights. Day one is usually spent meeting team members and management, finalizing any physical setup, and remaining paperwork. An HR staff member or co-worker is assigned to the new employee as a guide or mentor to walk the new hire throughout the day. The common activities include understanding the security arrangements within the company; finalizing paperwork; meeting team members and managers; finalizing equipment setup and access to networks; touring the workplace or virtual platforms; setting performance expectations; and understanding how it will be measured. As the orientation progresses, the newcomer is made to understand an overview of the company in terms of its history, mission, vision, and strategic goals; and code of conduct, benefits, safety protocols, and compliance training, with a view to establishing foundational knowledge and reinforcing company culture and values. Orientation is often characterized by office/facility tours; greeting and briefing from the leadership or HR; overview of the company policies and procedures; introduction to teams, etc.

First Week:

Steps must be taken to ensure that newcomers are not overloaded with information but are given time to learn about policies, procedures, and workflows. Therefore, orientation programs should be phased, and new entrants should take small, bite-sized tasks. It begins by introducing new employees to direct colleagues, with whom they have meetings, to learn more about what they do and how they will collaborate. The recruitment manager should also meet with new entrants to recap the first week, evaluate what went well and what could have been better, and see what's next. Other activities included a comprehensive overview of their job responsibilities, training sessions, and essential tools and systems they will be using. It is also very crucial to set clear targets at the onset for long-term success. The overall goal is to enable new entrants to have a helicopter view of role definitions, goal setting, explaining key performance indicators (KPIs), and starting off the process of assimilation into the company's culture and systems. In the first week, the new entrants continue to get familiar with the team, the company, and their role.

30-60-90-day plan:

It is important that new employees are made aware of their expectations in the first, second, and third months. The first 30 days are about getting employees to know the organization, complete orientation, take on-board modules regarding company policy, complete required compliance training, have a one-on-one meeting with a manager, and be assigned a mentor. This is the period when the new employees are encouraged to set three to five goals to achieve, connect with their team, and ask questions. The goals must be measurable so that employees will know when they have achieved them. The second month would launch the employees into role-specific activities, aimed at helping them have a more solid understanding of the fundamentals of the organization and its challenges. The new entrants are encouraged to work cross-departmentally and continue to take onboarding modules. At this point, they should become contributing members of their team. In the 90-day plan, the new entrants are effectively onboarded and integrated into the organization and its culture. Every new employee should be subjected to the 90-day onboarding process, irrespective of their previous experience, so that they can properly align with the new organization. The implication is that they will need guidance on how their behaviors can best contribute to the organizational strategy and which behaviors are the fastest and most likely to make the biggest impact. Therefore, the first 90 days are crucial for new entrants to be integrated into the company's culture and mesh with their team.

The goal is to establish the attitude of continuous learning and skill- building; regular feedback and adjustment, improve performance, and celebrate growth.

Role Training:

Onboarding training can take weeks and months and features prominently within the 30-60-90 onboarding plan. The training aspect is where onboarding becomes personalized. This phase is aimed at enabling new employees to acquire specific skills, tools, and knowledge needed to perform their jobs effectively. Job-specific training can be offered through lectures, seminars, workshops, manuals, and hands-on sessions tailored to the new employees' roles. In today's work environment, most of the onboarding trainings are offered digitally through webinars and virtual classrooms, e- learning modules, compliance training, micro learning, gamified, and simulation-based. Onboarding training covers performance management, especially in goal setting, measurement, and feedback, including the developmental programs that involve shadowing and mentoring, where new employees observe experienced colleagues and learn through guided practice (Jeske & Olson, 2021). Below is a breakdown of onboarding training content:

General Aspect: These include:

- The company's history, product, and competitors.
- Organizational mission, vision, and core values.
- Organizational culture and norms.
- Dress code, communication style, and meeting etiquette.
- General security matters, including fire, flood, and disasters, etc.

Terms and Conditions of Employment: These include

- Methods of remuneration.
- Working hours, break time, overtime, etc.
- Welfare–canteen, transport, medical, recreational facilities, toilet arrangements, etc.

Labor relations and employee discipline: These may include:

- Information about the labor unions in the organization.
- Code of conduct and behaviors that can lead to various kinds of discipline.
- Grievance procedure.
- Rules and regulations, etc.
- Career management: These include:
- Career pathing.
- Learning and development in the organization.
- E–learning modules.

Performance management: These may include:

- Goal setting, measurement, and feedback.
- Organizational structure and reporting relationship.
- Job description and key performance indicators.
- Security consciousness on the job.
- Waste prevention and productivity issues.
- Information about working tools.
- Job standards and standard practices.

Integration and engagement: These may include:

- Invitations to town halls, social events, or interest groups.

- Meet-and-greets or virtual coffee chats.
- Profiles of key executives and their roles.
- Assigning buddies for informal support.

Social Integration:

This is about assisting new entrants (within the 30-60-90-day plan) to have a sense of belonging, not only professionally, but also physically and emotionally connected to their job and the company. There are so many ways to help new employee's foster feelings of inclusiveness in an organization. This can be done by scheduling short introductory meeting lunches or virtual coffee chats with co-workers. Other ways could be by pairing new entrants with seasoned employees for guidance and camaraderie, including participating in events and traditions that define the company's identity. Additionally, the new members could be encouraged to get involved in involvement in ERGs (Employee Resource Groups), clubs, or Slack channels, by creating a more relaxed atmosphere for full participation. All these strategies will help foster cultural immersion, boosting engagement and morale; collaboration and trust; and reducing anxiety and the feeling of isolation.

At the end of the first year, the final stage of onboarding involves evaluation, revision, and ongoing support. Onboarding process and programs should be reviewed regularly through surveys and other feedback mechanisms, and revised accordingly when the need arises. This can be combined with the first annual performance review. Onboarding programs need to be updated regularly as internal processes and requirements change. Regular ongoing check-ins support would include supervisors meeting one-on-one with their employees weekly, and in the case of remote workers, it is important that the employees have a forum to talk informally. Furthermore, there should be open-door policies where employees are encouraged to contact managers with any concerns. Many organizations establish employee mental health plans and encourage work-life integration, as well as employee recognition programs that acknowledge great and outstanding achievements and thus boost employee morale. Other instruments that can be used to get important feedback to help new employees feel aligned and supported are pulse surveys and 360-degree feedback. While pulse surveys gauge satisfaction and identify gaps, 360-degree feedback gathers input from peers, mentors, and supervisors to provide a holistic view. In a nutshell, the final stage of the onboarding should be reviewing how the employees have fared in their first year and if they have met their long- term goals. It is important to align their preferences and career ambitions with the company's learning and development programs. Each phase of the onboarding process provides an opportunity to measure the effectiveness of your program by collecting and analyzing qualitative and quantitative data that would reveal important metrics relating to:

- Employee satisfaction level– the present health of your employee experience.
- Length of employees' stay in your organization or attrition rate.
- The length of time it takes for a new hire to start contributing to their team or the company overall (time-to-productivity).
- Tracking new employees to be sure that they are meeting onboarding milestones, such as completing compliance training (performance metrics).
- Interviewing those exiting on what would have made their onboarding a good experience (exit interview).

A smart onboarding system will track the effectiveness and efficiency of the onboarding process. However, beyond onboarding, organizations must pay attention to cross-boarding and off-boarding. Cross-boarding is the process of transitioning an existing employee into a new role or department within the same company and can be termed as the onboarding of existing employees or insiders. It involves training, upskilling, or reskilling of old employees in the organization so that they are empowered to take up new roles. However, these employees must be onboarded, equipped with the necessary skills and information about their new reporting structure, so that they are not overwhelmed by their new roles. Cross-boarding as part of the employee life cycle promotes internal mobility and career growth; reduces the cost of hiring new employees; and boosts employee engagement. On the other hand, offboarding is about some employees exiting the company, even after successful onboarding.

No matter what their reasons for leaving are, their departure must be handled with care, with the aim of creating a good impression. The first thing is trying to understand why they are exiting and to thank them for what they achieved while serving the company. It is also a good practice to say goodbye with warmth and some degree of affability, organize a farewell, and talk positively about them. Such last encounters can leave behind wonderful memories in the minds of exiting employees and make them become ambassadors for the company.

How to Create an Effective Onboarding:

Onboarding has become a strategic investment in people, and when done properly, it transforms new employees into loyal, high-performing members who understand how to contribute to the big picture and why it matters. However, creating an effective onboarding program starts with the unique needs of your company—from the type of employees you have hired (for example, remote vs. on-site, or full-time vs. part- time) to the culture of your company, which will affect the choices to be made. When these are well understood, onboarding can then serve as a bridge that turns potential into success in a world where culture and connection drive organizational success. Some of the highlights below may be useful in maximizing the potential in onboarding (Masoner, 2025; Reese, 2025):

Get Buy-in from leadership:

Notwithstanding that onboarding has a positive impact on retention, productivity, and engagement, sometimes it may struggle to gain traction without executive support. Hence HR department must help leadership understand the importance of an engaging, smooth, and inspiring onboarding experience. To convince leadership to invest in onboarding would mean that it must align with broader organizational goals and objectives, in terms of providing solutions to existing business challenges. There is no doubt that the executives respond to metrics, and for this reason, any case to be made must be backed up with compelling data that quantifies the impact of onboarding. For example, if leadership is interested in attrition level, show how onboarding reduces turnover rates among new employees, or improve other parameters such as productivity metrics, engagement scores, and cost of replacing a disengaged or undertrained employee. HR professionals can shift the conversation from the cost of onboarding to value addition, including intangible values. In addition, HR professionals can leverage industry research that shows how companies with structured onboarding programs outperform their peers in employee engagement and productivity. Beyond the presentation of data, tell a story that resonates by sharing real-life experiences of new employees who struggled due to a lack of onboarding, and compare it with the success stories of those who received onboarding. Leadership assurance is vital and can elevate onboarding from an HR initiative to a company-wide priority, but it must be well-designed, rolled out in phases, with resource requirements outlined, and show how technology would streamline delivery.

Identify what new hires need to succeed: Organizations employ different categories of employees whose job responsibilities, work environment, and accommodations may vary. When determining and codifying what new employees need, one may look at several factors and some of them are creating role outlines and guides for all job titles to address job-specifics; in terms of technology and equipment, your warehouse workers may need personal safety equipment (PSE); and all new employees, no matter their previous experience should undergo one form of training or the other to meet company specific procedures.

Plan your logistics:

Having identified the need, they must be codified, adequate resources provided, and assigned to individuals for implementation. It is important to determine who owns each step in the onboarding process for each job title; who is the coordinator of the whole process; and set a timeline for each step.

Automating onboarding programs:

Automating onboarding is not about replacing the human touch, but about increasing HR efficiency, saving time and cost, and giving real-time tracking and insight into the onboarding process. It streamlines onboarding, personalizes new employees' experience, and frees up human resources to focus on other matters. Automation can handle repetitive tasks such as sending welcome messages and instructional emails at intervals during preloading to engage employees early without overwhelming them with information, and with efficiency and consistency. It can provide self- services to new employees; notify other employees involved in the onboarding when they need to take action; and schedule surveys at intervals, following the 30-60-90-day plan. In addition, smart systems can personalize onboarding programs to new entrants based on job role, location, and experience level, and this is contrary to the myth that automation is impersonal. One of the advantages of automation is that it is scalable and can adapt to changing needs, as well as integrate with other platforms and evolve with the organization.

Culture assimilation:

Onboarding is not the sole responsibility of the HR department, though they play a critical part; it is the responsibility of the entire organization. Managers, supervisors, and co- workers play vital roles in instilling the company's culture; they help new employees understand the company culture, educate them on the company history, and explain company values and expected behaviors. They provide information and guidance to newcomers to assist them in adjusting to their work environment. When newcomers come to the workplace and begin to interact with existing or old staff, without concerted effort, they tend to learn the norms of the workgroup and the culture of the organization. In essence, for cultural assimilation to be effective, new employees must have some team members they can rely on to ask questions and help them settle in. Launch and other forms of recreation could be organized. This gives the team a chance to unwind together and interact with their new colleague in a relaxed and friendly environment. In fact, in some organizations, new employees are paired with the old ones (buddy system), with a view to sharing knowledge and helping the newcomer settle down as quickly as possible. During the onboarding process, senior leaders are called upon to talk about the company's vision, mission, and core values; lead tours of the building or facility; facilitate specific training, and even take newcomers out for coffee or lunch.

Emphasize the company's values and vision: Introducing new employees to the mission, goals, and values of the company is one of the most important parts of the employee orientation process, as it provides the reasons why the company exists, where it has come from, and where it is headed. In fact, the onboarding of new staff should center on practical knowledge, skills, and competency, and a clear-cut understanding of the organizational culture, ethics, and core values (Hendricks and Louw-Potgieter, 2012).

Attention to legal requirements:

Every company is required to stay compliant with relevant regulations and guidelines. New employees in the US must be conversant in laws and regulations on: Family and Medical Leave Act (FMLA); Americans with Disabilities Act (ADA); Fair Labor Standards Act (FLSA); Title VII of the Civil Rights Act of 1964; Age Discrimination in Employment Act (ADEA), etc.

Outline company expectations clearly:

Although the new employees' job description will carry some of the details, it is important to lead each employee through the expectations you have for them, along with why they are important to the company's success. For example, if you have a policy around booking leave in advance, ensure you explain the policy on attendance, performance management, leave/absence, career path, etc.

Follow up regularly:

For best practice, each phase of the onboarding process must be reviewed to ensure that the program is on course. Usually, face-to-face meetings are scheduled with the new employee after a few weeks, with the aim of finding out what is going on with them, what challenges they have found in integrating with your team, etc. It is vital in those early days that you are easily accessible by any new employee, so that the employee can easily verify issues of concern. It is good to ask a new employee for feedback from time to time to ascertain if it is achieving its purpose. This will also reveal where to make further improvements. Probably the easiest way to check the effectiveness of your induction process is to ask people who have just finished their onboarding programs what they think about it. This feedback will be an invaluable source of information and will allow you to tweak your onboarding process so that you can continually improve. For example, these three questions normally yield some good answers.

- What is something you wish we had explained better in this onboarding?
- What is one piece of advice you would give to the next person who is hired?
- How could we have done a better job on your onboarding process? What could be improved?

Other areas organizations should pay attention to are retention rates among new staff to see if there is a pattern of people leaving within a year of taking the job. If you have a high turnover of new staff, this will indicate that something is amiss, and changes may be needed. This gives you great feedback to consider and include in your future onboarding process, as your team grows. A successful employee onboarding program provides a chance for organizations to easily sell themselves to new employees. If done correctly, it can significantly increase the retention of staff and reduce the time it takes for a new employee to settle into their new work environment (Gibbons, 2025).

The importance of onboarding:

Onboarding prepares the stage for employees' first contact with their organization and sets the tone for the entire employee life cycle. According to Gallup (2021), employees who experience excellent onboarding are 2.6 times more likely to be extremely satisfied at work.

In the same vein, an effective onboarding process can boost employee retention by 82% and increase productivity by over 70% (TeamOut, 2025). Despite the huge benefits of employee onboarding, the process may not yield the desired result unless it is properly designed and implemented. HBR Survey (2023) indicates that about 52% of new hires were satisfied with their onboarding experience; 32% of the new hires found the whole experience confusing, while 22% of the new hires surveyed felt their onboarding was downright disorganized. This finding underlines the importance of effective employee onboarding that is strategically oriented, aimed at shaping employees' experience, to accelerate productivity and strengthen organizational culture, while avoiding disengagement, early turnover, and cultural disconnect. A well-structured onboarding will deliver quantifiable benefits in these areas:

Retention and morale:

The hiring process is demanding on both the employer and the employee. Most new employees will start a new job with high levels of motivation and will be keen to demonstrate to their new employers that they are the right person for the job. However, without an effective onboarding process, the journey for the new employee can be fraught with danger. The new employee will not be aware of the culture of a company, why things are done differently, why people laugh at jokes that weren't funny at their last job, how to approach people when problems arise, etc. Task-related issues will also compound the problem, and eventually, the new employee will lack confidence, which could be interpreted by their peers as a lack of competence. This is a downward spiral that will be difficult to reverse and ultimately may lead to the new employees walking out the door and not coming back. According to Deloitte (2023), a well-designed, strategic onboarding program plays a crucial role in the employees' experience, because workers who feel that their onboarding is highly effective are 18 times more likely to feel highly committed to their organization. Deloitte concludes that 69% of employees are more likely to stay with the company if they have a positive onboarding experience. On the other hand, early turnover can be very costly to organizations that have invested in recruitment and perhaps initial training without receiving productive contributions from their employees. To reduce high turnover and low employee morale, organizations should focus on creating strategic onboarding that reduces early departure risk and builds a foundation for long-term success. When new entrants are integrated with their organizations, this can result in much higher retention and greater savings by cutting turnover costs.

Productivity:

From a business point of view, productivity should be a fundamental point to consider in the hiring process. Nobody expects the new person to slot straight in and to be as productive as an experienced employee, but there should be an expectation that they will learn quickly and become productive in as short a time frame as possible. Shortcuts and incorrect work practices will undoubtedly lead to a loss of productivity. However, an effective onboarding process should seek to teach people the right way of doing things from the beginning. An onboarding program is part of an organization's knowledge management process and is intended to enable the new starter to become a useful and integrated member of the team. The overall goal of onboarding is to help new employees learn about the organization as soon as possible so that they can begin contributing. A good onboarding program covers all aspects of the company's operations and helps new employees become familiar with the organization's work culture, vision, mission, and goals. At the same time, new employees understand their roles in achieving the company's goals. This will help enhance the efficiency of employees, who need to adjust to the work culture of the organization and get involved in their jobs. Overall, it greatly helps increase the operational efficiency of the organization (Brodie, 2006; Derven, 2008). According to

MATCHR (2025), organizations with standardized onboarding processes see a 54% increase in productivity among new employees. Therefore, well- designed onboarding aimed at improving performance must:

- Provide clarity by outlining performance expectations, workflow, and measurement standards. This clarity drives confidence, eliminates ambiguity, and empowers employees to put in their best.
- Reduce mistakes by ensuring employees understand their roles, tools, and responsibilities.
- Build collaboration by connecting new employees with mentors, supervisors, managers, and peers; and creating a support system, which in turn fosters learning and integration and reduces burnout.
- Foster continuous learning and feedback by providing ongoing learning and performance check-ins to ensure that employees refine their skills and meet expectations.

Compliance:

In today's workplace, compliance is not just an obligation but a strategic imperative. Onboarding is important for legal reasons because, as an employer, you are obliged to make sure your employees are trained to do their jobs safely and know what to do in the event of a fire or other emergency. There is a saying- "ignorance of the law is not an excuse", a legal principle which means that a person or organization that claims ignorance of the law may not escape liability for violating that law. Businesses are expected to comply with regulations and legislation in areas such as data privacy, workplace safety, and environmental management. An effective employee onboarding process should seek to educate new employees about company policies and procedures and ethical standards, which may lead to unnecessary vulnerabilities and possible litigation or penalties. In essence, helps organizations to reduce risk exposure and empowers employees to act responsibly. Therefore, onboarding serves to:

- Educate employees on company policies, legal obligations, and industry regulations.
- Clarify roles and responsibilities in the aviation industry, healthcare, and manufacturing industries.
- Establish behavioral expectations that support equal employment, diversity, equity, and inclusion, anti-harassment, cybersecurity, and reporting protocols.
- Foster psychological safety, where employees feel safe to ask questions and report concerns, without victimization.
- Develop a compliance mindset that is required in getting things right.

Reputation:

A company's reputation is vital to its well-being, especially in this era of social media. A well-executed onboarding program can promote a company's reputation, attract top talent, and foster long-term loyalty. It does this by helping to shape the first impression that a new employee may have of a business, and this, in turn, will influence future recruitment drives. For example, employees frequently share their companies and their onboarding experiences on platforms like Glassdoor, LinkedIn, and Indeed. What it means is that a negative review from a disillusioned new hire can deter future candidates and cause damage to the employer's credibility. Therefore, the way a company welcomes and integrates new entrants speaks volumes. The best candidates will delve a little deeper into the company website when researching for positions to see what their employees' experiences look like. A company that provides a well-thought-out and structured onboarding program will more than likely perform well across other areas of business, such as customer service. Therefore, companies should pay attention to external and internal reputation. A good external reputation will help organizations attract the best talent in a competitive market space. These candidates are drawn to the company on account of its reputation and its organizational processes, which may be perceived as well-organized, employee-centric, and trustworthy. On the other hand, a poor reputation may hurt a company's recruitment drive, increase hiring costs, and reduce the quality of applicants. The internal reputation may consist of how employees perceive management and leadership styles, HR, and the organization's values. If a new entrant gets adequate support from the organization, they would more likely trust the company and become its ambassadors. This singular goodwill can translate to stronger collaboration and higher employee engagement. Certainly, onboarding will contribute a great deal to how employees talk about their workplace, perceive its brand, and how the broader market evaluates the organization's integrity.

Employee engagement:

Onboarding is one of the critical drivers of employee engagement. Employee engagement is the emotional and physical connection an employee has toward their organization and its goals, and involves how new hires perceive their roles, their teams, and the company culture. A robust onboarding program is an excellent way of facilitating employee engagement. Engaged employees are more committed, productive, and likely to stay with the organization for a longer period, while the cost of Ineffective onboarding, on the flip side, can lead to disengagement, low productivity, and high turnover rates. Furthermore, disengaged employees can negatively impact team morale and overall organizational performance. According to SHRM (2025), 81% of HR professionals are of the view that increasing employee engagement is a top-three priority. Onboarding drives employee engagement in a number of ways:

- Creating a sense of belonging and organizational identification: Effective onboarding is a strategic lever for cultivating social bonding and team dynamics, which invariably helps new employee understand their place within the organizational structure. When a new entrant feels welcomed and valued, they are more likely to identify with the company's objectives and goals. Fostering a sense of belonging and identification strengthens emotional commitment, reduces turnover and burnout, thereby promoting employee engagement.

- Clarity of roles and expectations: Onboarding provides role-specific guidance and expectations that foster engagement. This clarity about employees' responsibilities, performance measurement, and career pathing empowers them to take ownership of their work, become invested, and align their efforts with organizational objectives.
- Cultural immersion: Onboarding introduces you to the norms, values, and behaviors that define the workplace. By resonating with the company culture, values, mission, and policies, they are to be authentically engaged and contribute positively to team dynamics.
- Co-worker integration and collaboration: As new employees integrate with the company, they also interact with managers and peers, laying the foundation for trust and collaboration. Specific onboarding relating to mentorship, team-building activities, and peer support accelerates social integration, which is a key driver of engagement.
- Job satisfaction: When employees feel valued and supported from the start, they tend to stick with the company, leading to higher job satisfaction and a deeper commitment to the organization.

Time and money-saving:

One of the most valuable resources of any organization is time. Onboarding plays a significant role in saving the time of the organization by directly influencing how quickly new hires become productive contributors (SHRM, 2022). Employee onboarding is one of the ways to optimize operational efficiency. The strategic aim goes beyond introducing entrants to the workplace to improving productivity, reducing turnover, training redundancies, and recruitment costs. It does this by streamlining training modules so as to reduce repetitive instruction; setting clear expectations to minimize confusion and delays; and early integration of new employees into teams, to speed up collaboration and workflow. Onboarding training provides new entrants with all the information needed to start performing their duties as quickly as possible, and this saves time and money. Many companies have discovered that the cost of not training is higher than the cost of training, and hence, there is a higher risk of choosing not to train new employees into the business. Successful onboarding programs can also lead to cost savings (Cooper-Thomas & Anderson, 2006). The indirect costs of early departure of a newly hired executive (Wells, 2005) or labor turnover (Derven, 2008; Friedman, 2006) could be reduced by a good onboarding program. On the other hand, the direct cost of an onboarding program could be reduced by automating the process (Butler, 2008).

The financial implications of poor onboarding could be huge because the cost of getting it wrong is far greater than the investment required to get it right. According to SHRM (2008), the cost of replacing an employee can range from

50% to 200% of their annual salary, depending on the role and organizational context. Hence, investment in onboarding can serve a strategic purpose in reducing ramp-up time for new hires, lowering recruitment and training costs, and above all, enhancing employee satisfaction, which leads to better performance and innovation. There are many benefits associated with onboarding that cannot be easily quantified: It reinforces a new employee's decision to join the organization and fosters a feeling of belonging. A well- organized onboarding program will aid staff in dealing with anxiety by providing them with coping strategies like goal setting and planning during one of the most stressful times in their organizational life. By reducing insecurity and anxiety, onboarding programs can help employees settle in faster and feel more at home in the organization.

These positive emotions may lead to improved levels of satisfaction amongst new employees, which in turn could translate into a more productive workforce, well-prepared to beat the competition.

Phases of Socialization Process:

Organizational socialization is a dynamic process through which individual's transition from outsiders to integrated members of a workplace. It involves the acquisition of knowledge and skills, as well as the internalization of norms, values, and identity. Many researches abound on the subject, such as Buchanan (1974),

Wanous (1978), Feldman (1981), Allen and Meyer (1990), etc. However, we shall use the foundational theory from Jablin (1987), titled "Contemporary Research and Practical Implications for onboarding, Role Development, and Offboarding", to illustrate the stages or processes involved in organizational socialization. Fredric Jablin, in his work, outlines four key phases: anticipatory socialization, encounter, change & acquisition, and exit & disengagement, each representing a distinct psychological and behavioral shift in the employee lifecycle.

Anticipatory Socialization:

This can be referred to as a pre-arrival stage. This stage occurs before new hires join the organization. Through interacting with representatives of the company (e.g., recruiters, managers), new hires develop expectations about the company and the job prior to organizational entry. It recognizes the fact that all new entrants are coming in with a set of values, attitudes, expectations, and learning. Anticipatory socialization refers to all the learning that has taken place before the new person joins an organization. Therefore, as they come to know about the organization and their jobs during the selection process, they form expectations and impressions about what membership in an organization is like. Their information source may come from the internet, employment recruiters, advertisements, rumors, etc. People's impressions and expectations can attract them to one organization or the other. It is at this stage that individuals assess the extent to which their skills, abilities, needs, and values match those they perceive the organization may require or prefer. It is therefore very important for recruiters/managers not to exaggerate the conditions of employment but give accurate information to prospective job seekers to correct their inaccurate expectations to avoid the negative consequences for performance, satisfaction, and tenure (attrition). Organizations can shape anticipatory socialization through realistic job previews, transparent recruitment messaging, and value-based branding. Any misalignment between expectations and reality often leads to early dissatisfaction or turnover. This phase ends when the new worker is employed, which is the period when the hiring process is completed.

Encounter:

As new employees enter an organization and start playing their role, they begin to compare their expectations, the image of the company, and the reality on the ground. If expectation and reality match, the encounter would be smooth. When the two are at variance, stress and frustration set in. This will generate a mental process of adjustment, whereby the individual tries to replace his own values and norms with those of the organization. On the other hand, if he cannot reconcile with the organizational norms and values, he will get disillusioned. At this stage, expectations can be confirmed or rejected. For example, if an employee joins a company with the expectation that the promotion will be rapid, this may lead to some unpleasant surprise if, in reality, it is not so. Many newcomers experience reality shock when their expectations are unmet, regardless of how unrealistic those expectations may be. Newcomers who experience these surprises would try to make sense of them. Based on their own predispositions and past experiences and based on how others within and outside the organization interpret these surprises, the sense-making process can help a newcomer resolve unmet expectations. Individuals whose sense-making complements the organization are more likely to stay with that organization. It is a very crucial stage that new employees manage to resolve conflicts between lifestyle and within the workgroup, and become familiar with the dynamics of the job and workgroup. The strategic implication for HR practitioners is to design effective onboarding programs, coaching, mentoring, and early feedback to reduce uncertainty and accelerate adjustment. This is because the quality of the encounter phase strongly predicts long-term engagement and performance. The phase is crucial for some reasons:

- It is the phase that new employees try to understand their company, the rules and regulations, their responsibilities, and how it contributes to the big picture.
- It is a phase where new entrants try to get feedback from their team members as an evaluation that gives them an understanding of their level of competence in that particular job position.
- It is a phase of cultivating a relationship with co-

workers and receiving social and emotional support.

Change Acquisition:

The final stage of socialization generally recognizes successful adjustment as an organizational newcomer is transformed into an organizational insider. Insiders have learned the ropes to fit in and can serve as valuable resources of information for future newcomers. This stage can also be referred to as the stage of settling in or metamorphosis. This occurs when the new entrants have adjusted to organizational norms and values and mastered the task they must perform. At this stage, change has taken place. The new employee is now compatible with the organization. This marks the completion of socialization. Employees who have successfully undergone these three processes are more likely to be satisfied, internally motivated, committed to their job, and may remain with the organization. This stage is marked out by some of these features:

- New members become comfortable with the organization and their team.
- New members feel competent to complete their jobs successfully.
- They understand the organizational system, and not only their own tasks but also the rules and procedures.
- Productivity will improve, alongside commitment.

The strategic implication is that as new employees begin to master required tasks, internalize organizational norms, and develop a stable role identity, it behooves HR leaders to support them with continuous learning, provide developmental feedback, and encourage autonomy. Other exposures employees may require at this phase would be to introduce them to stretch assignments, leadership development, and cross-functional activities.

Organizational Socialization Tactics:

Organizations rely on a variety of tactics to help newcomers fit in, and they do so by leveraging the seminal work of Maanen and Schein (1979), who identified six sets of tactics that organizations can adopt to socialize their employees. These tactics are key to how new entrants feel and perform their work, and to understanding how to develop a long- term relationship between the organization and its employees during the tenure of their employment. To ensure the success of employee adjustment, Maanen and Schein identified six different tactical socialization dimensions: collective vs. individual, formal vs. informal, sequential vs. random steps, fixed vs. variable, serial vs. disjunctive, and investiture vs. divestiture. Each set of tactics represents a continuum between institutionalized (structured, organization-driven) and individualized (flexible, newcomer-driven) approaches. These tactics are often embedded in formal onboarding programs and leadership pipelines, bearing in mind that employee socialization is a complex process that requires a multifaceted approach. As newcomers assume duty, they face uncertainty and the need to adapt. This journey involves developing clear role expectations, empowering individuals to act with confidence, and fostering meaningful social integration within the organizational context. Successful socialization leads to improved adjustment, knowledge, and confidence, depending on the choice of tactics deployed by the organization. However, a good socialization strategy would blend different approaches to achieve employee engagement, job satisfaction, and improved performance. Good socialization strategies mix different approaches.

Collective vs. Individual:

Collective socialization refers to the tactic of putting new employees through a common set of experiences, not as individuals but as a group. A good example is a cohort of new hires attending a standardized orientation program; basic training of new recruits in a military organization; training a group of salesmen in an organization, etc. On the other hand, individual socialization is the tactic of giving an employee a unique set of experiences, singularly and in isolation. For instance, an onboarding program can be designed for a particular manager based on the unique role he or she is to play in that organization, or he/she may undergo on-the-job training, coaching, and mentoring programs. Some advantages are associated with both practices, while collective socialization promotes uniformity, shared identity, solidarity, and reduces ambiguity within the cohort group being socialized; individualized socialization encourages personalization.

Overall, individual processes are expensive both in time and money and most likely to be associated with complex roles and may increase uncertainty and role ambiguity.

Table 4.3: Key Differences between Collective and Individual Socialization

Feature	Collective Socialization	Individual Socialization
Format	Group-based	One-on-one
Consistency	High across participants	Variable, role-specific
Efficiency	Time- and cost-efficient	Resource-intensive
Social Support	Peer bonding and shared experience	Relies on a mentor or supervisor
Flexibility	Low	High
Feature	Collective Socialization	Individual Socialization
Risk of Isolation	Low	Higher if not well-supported

Formal vs. Informal:

Formal socialization refers to the tactic in which newcomers are more or less segregated from regular organizational members while undergoing a set of experiences tailored explicitly for them. In other words, new employees are clearly distinguished from existing employees during onboarding sessions. A formal socialization is a structured and intentional process by which individuals learn the culture, values, roles, and expectations of a specific organization; and such a process is guided by authority figures like managers, supervisors, teachers, etc., with clearly defined goals, rules, and curricula; and in a controlled environment. These processes are illustrated by such socialization processes taking place in educational settings, workplace onboarding, military training, religious institutions, government, or civic programs. It is typically found in organizations where specific preparation for new positions is involved and where it is deemed important that a newcomer learn the official and acceptable attitudes, values, and protocol associated with the new role. Formal socialization may be associated with hierarchical boundaries, wherein a new employee is expected to assume a new status or rank in the organization, while on the flip side, informal socialization is most likely to be associated with functional boundaries, wherein the newcomer must learn new skills, methods, or practical abilities. Additionally, formal socialization becomes imperative where the nature of work involves a high level of risk to the new employee, co-workers, the organization itself, and/or clients of the organization. Hence, the training and socialization period of pilots, doctors, engineers, and other professionals is usually long in order to avoid mistakes and penalties arising therefrom.

Informal socialization, in contrast, is the unstructured and spontaneous process by which individuals learn the culture, values, roles, and expectations of a specific organization, outside of the formal settings, in an unplanned and organic manner; peer-driven, subtle, and ongoing. The socialization is organic and occurs naturally through everyday interactions, observations, and experiences, including learning on the job, shadowing colleagues, and often without formal training or explicit instruction. It can have a more profound effect in shaping the identity and behavior of individuals than the formal process because it involves on-the-job contingencies as well as teaching by people who are clearly doing the work. Some examples include picking up on unwritten rules like dress code or email etiquette; learning social boundaries through group interactions or peer feedback; and adjusting to new cultural environments when traveling or relocating.

Table 4.4: Key Differences between Formal and Informal Socialization:

Feature	Formal Socialization	Informal Socialization
Structure	Highly organized and planned	Unstructured and spontaneous
Authority	Guided by designated leaders	Peer or family-driven
Evaluation	Often includes assessments or feedback	Rarely evaluated formally
Goal Orientation	Aligns with institutional objectives	Emerges from daily life experiences
Examples	School, onboarding, religious rites	Peer influence, family habits, and media

Sequential vs. Random Socialization Tactics:

Sequential socialization refers to the extent to which clear steps or stages are established to assist a new employee in understanding their roles. Each of the stages is built upon the previous to provide clarity and a roadmap for progression. For example, a person being prepared for medical practice may have to go through an undergraduate pre-med program, medical school, internship, and residency, and specialist board examinations before becoming a medical doctor. Similarly, a person wishing to become a Managing Director may have to rotate through several positions to build experience and a track record. This tactic is employed in organizations that are interested in defining their milestones, setting clear expectations and timelines, and establishing feedback loops aligned to each stage of the socialization. In contrast, random socialization lacks prescribed order and occurs when the sequence of steps leading to the target role is unknown, ambiguous, or continually changing. The learning experience of new employees is often in an unpredictable sequence and shaped by situational demands and informal interactions. Some of its main characteristics are unpredictable learning experience, unclear roles and fluid expectations, and too much reliance on informal networks and self-direction. Random tactic is prevalent in startups, IT and creative industries, and other roles requiring high autonomy.

Though sequential socialization, when compared with random socialization, may stifle innovation and adaptability because of its bureaucratic setup, it can help organizations reduce ambiguity and anxiety for new employees, enhance role clarity and performance readiness, and facilitate standardized cultural transmission. On the other hand, new employees who encounter socialization in a random fashion develop initiative and problem-solving skills, foster innovation and rapid adaptation, including customization based on individual strengths. In a fast-changing world, a company that wants to groom top organizational leaders should reflect deeply on its organizational values and strategic priorities because sequential and random socialization tactics are not merely operational choices; they are strategic levers that shape how individuals engage, adapt, and contribute within organizations. The choice between sequential and random socialization depends on organizational priorities. For instance, if the organization wants to raise innovative managers, the approach would be to reduce sequential processes and include more random socialization experience, and by so doing, the onboarding program would be crafted to balance clarity with creativity, encouraging new employees to refine or reshape their roles.

Fixed vs. Variable Socialization:

This dimension refers to the degree to which the steps involved in a socialization process have a clearly defined timetable that is both adhered to by the new employee and the organization. Newcomers are informed in advance of how long each phase of the socialization would take, when the transition would occur, and the expected milestones to be achieved. For instance, when this approach is embedded into onboarding programs, some management trainees may be given rotational assignments to help them gain specific knowledge within a fixed time. Similarly, lecturers in the academic environment may have to stay a certain number of years, teach a certain number of hours, and publish a certain number of articles before being promoted to the next rank. In a nutshell, fixed socialization is time-bound, with clear start and end points, structured progression, and predictable feedback and evaluation schedules. This approach helps to reduce ambiguity and anxiety for new employees, which are crucial for roles requiring precision and compliance; enhances psychological safety and role clarity, as well as standardizes cultural transmission and compliance.

On the other hand, variable socialization tactic lacks a predetermined timeline as new employees have less clue as to when to expect a given boundary passage. The duration and pacing of socialization depend on individual performance, situational demands, or organizational discretion. Some of the key characteristics are that the approach is open-ended or with a fluid timeline, progression is based on readiness and not based on calendar dates, and it is marked with internal feedback and evolving expectations. This tactic is common in fast-changing environments where flexibility, innovation, and personalized development are prioritized. It allows for personalized learning, autonomy, and initiatives, and adapts to changing organizational needs or individual capabilities. Both fixed and variable socializations come with their unique impacts, and the implication for HR practitioners is to leverage this tactic by blending both approaches when designing onboarding programs to achieve maximum results. For example, the fixed approach can be used to encourage consistency and accountability and to reinforce shared values and norms, while the variable tactic can be deployed to reveal unique strengths and growth paths and to foster creativity and innovation.

Serial vs Disjunctive Socialization:

Serial socialization refers to where a newcomer (who is about to assume a position in an organization) is trained by an experienced employee (who has been in that position or is currently an incumbent, now serving as mentor or role model). This dimension plays a pivotal role in shaping how newcomers interpret their roles, internalize culture, and develop professional identity. The role model serves as a behavioral template, offering insights, feedback, and cultural cues that help newcomers navigate their new environment. It is simply characterized by the presence of a designated mentor or predecessor; structured guidance and modelling of expected behaviors; and ensuring continuity between past and present role occupants.

In contrast, disjunctive socialization occurs when a new employee enters roles without guidance from a predecessor or mentor. Put differently, it is a situation where newcomers are not following the footsteps of immediate or recent predecessors, or where no role model is available to show newcomers how to proceed in the new role, and for this reason, the socialization process becomes disjunctive. It is characterized by an absence of a role model, high autonomy, and self- directed learning, and role ambiguity and open-ended expectations. This approach is common in newly created positions, startups, or during organizational re-engineering. The implication is that new employees are expected to interpret expectations, build relationships, and define their role independently. The presence or absence of role models significantly influences newcomer adjustment; hence, HR leaders can design tailored integration experiences that balance tradition with transformation, ultimately driving both alignment and innovation.

Investiture vs Divestiture Socialization:

Investiture recognizes personal identity, values, and other characteristics that a new employee brings to work. It affirms and reinforces the unique skills and knowledge that the employees bring with them to the organization, rather than treating new employees as people who come with nothing. This tactic encourages them to integrate their unique perspectives into the organization. Validating prior experience and identity enhances psychological safety and inclusion, engagement, and job satisfaction and fosters cultural integration through mutual respect. For example, during onboarding new employee may be invited to share their past experiences and contribute to process improvement.

On the other hand, the divestiture socialization process seeks to deny and strip the new employee of their prior identity to fully adopt the norms, values, and behaviors of the organization. This approach is commonly employed in professions or institutions with tightly held cultural values, like military organizations, religious communities, or elite professional training environments that rely on this tactic to reinforce conformity and reshape individual identity. For instance, a military institution may require new cadets to pass through rigorous training that strips away their civilian habits in order to instill a new professional identity. Both investiture and divestiture socialization represent powerful dimensions for shaping how new employees experience organizational entry. HR leaders can strategically design an onboarding program that balances authenticity with alignment, fostering both inclusion and performance. The approaches are critical to shaping psychological safety and long-term engagement.

Outcomes of Organizational Socialization:

Organizational socialization is the process through which new employees acquire knowledge and skills, attitudes and behavior, and cultural norms necessary to function effectively within a workplace. They are equally critical, shaping not only individual performance and well-being but also broader organizational effectiveness. Socializing in today's organizations has changed, and the advantages are clear. People are more connected than ever, mixing and mingling in new ways through technological advancement, remote work, and varied workforce interactions, and organizations that overlook these essential processes face disengagement, elevated turnover, and weak team unity. Conversely, successful socialization techniques come with multiple dividends such as heightened job satisfaction, greater organizational loyalty, enhanced interpersonal connections, and improved overall performance, etc. (Mahmud, 2025; Houle et al, 2024; Baur & Erdogan, 2011). Hence, employee socialization acts as a key resource for lasting organizational achievements, and a few of them are discussed below:

Job Satisfaction:

This is defined as the level of contentment employees feel with their job or the positive emotional response employees experience on their job, and these can sometimes be difficult to measure quantitatively. However, proactive organizations apply a mixed method of research to determine the satisfaction level of their employees on several organizational issues, including employee socialization programs. Job satisfaction stands out as a central indicator of successful socialization programs when it is thoughtfully designed and strategically implemented to foster role clarity, belongingness, and empowerment. These dimensions shape how employees perceive their roles, relationships, and organizational culture. Job satisfaction is a multifaceted construct that goes beyond employees' daily duties to include relationships with team members/managers, the challenging nature of the job (Is it pushing employees to new heights), satisfaction with organizational policies, satisfaction with the career progression, and the impact of their job on employees' personal lives. While many factors contribute to employee job satisfaction, three psychological constructs have emerged as the outcome of successful organizational socialization, namely, role clarity, self-efficacy, and social acceptance.

Role clarity refers to the extent to which new employees understand their job responsibilities, performance expectations, including measurement and feedback, and the reporting relationships. Some of the goals of the socialization process are to aid newcomers in reducing uncertainty, making it easier for them to get their jobs done correctly and efficiently. It also enhances the confidence of the new entrants in decision-making and task prioritization, while fostering a sense of control and predictability, which contributes to psychological comfort. At times, there may be a disconnect between the main responsibilities listed in job descriptions and the specific things to be done. It is during socialization that managers take time to explain exactly what is expected. An ineffective socialization program may produce employees who exhibit poor performance because they are unsure of their exact roles and responsibilities. A strong socialization program, all things being equal, would produce employees who are productive and understand what is expected of them. Organizations benefit from increasing role clarity for a new employee. Not only does role clarity imply greater job satisfaction and organizational commitment, but it is also linked to productivity. Here, the strategic implication for HR leaders is to ensure that socialization programs, job descriptions, performance indicators, and managerial feedback emphasize clarity from the onset, as role ambiguity could be a precursor to dissatisfaction and disengagement (Bauer et al. 2007; Chao et al. 1994).

Self-efficacy is a psychological concept first explored by Albert Bandura of a person's belief in his/her ability to successfully perform a task and overcome challenges. It is the confidence we have in ourselves to plan and execute a course of action to achieve a specific outcome. According to Bandura (1977), there are four critical factors that contribute to one's self-efficacy, namely mastery experiences, vicarious experiences, verbal persuasion, and physiological and affective states. Your previous success in doing something is an indication that you can succeed in a similar situation, but if you have not succeeded in the past, you may doubt your ability because a lack of cogent experience can lead to low self-efficacy. In other words, the absence of any past reference points can make you feel uncertain about how your skills will align with a task. Similarly, seeing people around you succeed gives you the confidence that success is possible, whereas if what you hear or see is how people failed in their endeavors, this can be very discouraging and cast doubt on whether or not your skills are enough to break the pattern of defeat. Also, the kind of feedback one receives matters a great deal: positive feedback and providing suggestions on how to improve, including celebrating one's success, can build self-efficacy, and on the flipside, harsh criticisms, verbal abuse, and insults can damage self- esteem, lower self-belief, and above all, create a sense of inadequacy. Lastly, a person's mental and physical state is very crucial: if you feel weak, fatigued, ill, stressed, traumatized, or have a negative mental state, all these can contribute to low self-efficacy. The takeaway for HR professionals is built upon socialization programs that support mastery through scaffolded learning, early wins, and affirming feedback. As a source of motivation, employees with high self-efficacy should be encouraged, and at the same time, attempts should be made to reduce situations that cause stress and burnout, discrimination and harassment, and negative mental health conditions. Building employees' self-efficacy, confidence, self-esteem, and positive mindset positively affects their job satisfaction.

The next sub-topic to consider, which invariably improves job satisfaction, is social acceptance. This is to the extent to which one feels integrated within the social fabric of the environment. In other words, it is the degree to which employees feel welcomed, valued, and included by peers, supervisors, and within a broader organizational culture. Social acceptance gives new employees the support needed to be successful. For socialization to be effective, employees must interact with other coworkers and supervisors socially and involve themselves in functions involving other employees. Social acceptance is linked to affective commitment, which is a key driver of employee satisfaction (Allen & Meyer, 1990), and leads to higher satisfaction among employees when it affirms their identity and fosters inclusion (Yu, 2020). Therefore, social acceptance impacts employees' job satisfaction when it emotionally connects them to their work and minimizes the feeling of isolation; when it enhances collaboration, psychological safety, a sense of belongingness, and trust; and when it reinforces identity alignment. HR leaders should leverage socialization, particularly the investiture tactic, to validate employees' identity, create peer networks, and affinity groups to promote belongingness and relatedness in a social environment. This is crucial because when employees feel that their perspectives and values are respected, there is a greater tendency for them to experience emotional alignment with the organization.

Strategically, every aspect of employee socialization can be prioritized to increase job satisfaction. For example, during the anticipatory stage, if HR managers ensure that their recruitment messages are not exaggerated, this will help align job candidates' expectations with organizational realities, and this singular action can minimize cognitive dissonance and disappointment, and lay the foundation for job satisfaction. Also, during the encounter and acquisition stage, timely and constructive feedback can go a long way to reinforce progress and confidence. Note that if early wins are recognized and celebrated, they can contribute to a sense of accomplishment and satisfaction. Socialization tactics could be harped on. Consider serial socialization, where new employees are guided by mentors; these experienced individuals not only transmit knowledge, but also foster trust, psychological safety, and encouragement, which in turn enhances affective satisfaction. Others like sequential and fixed socialization tactics play a great role in reinforcing satisfaction, especially when learning programs are phased, with milestone-based feedback, they provide predictability and support that make employees feel competent and cared for.

Performance and Innovation:

Performance refers to how efficiently and effectively an organization uses its resources to achieve its stated goals. It is the extent to which employees execute their roles effectively in meeting expectations and contributing to the goal of the organization, while innovation consists of the generation and implementation of new ideas, processes, and solutions. The basic purpose of every organization is to make the new employees industrious as soon as possible. The knowledge that should be imparted to new employees includes organizational culture and ethics. The new employee must understand the company's values, goals, roles, norms, and overall work environment. The culture of an organization influences the way people dress and behave. It allows for social acceptance and aids in completing tasks in a way that meets company standards.

Understanding of the company's culture increases employee commitment and satisfaction.

Hence, detailed information relating to work is provided at the initial stage itself. Information relating to rules and policies helps employees to have a good understanding of the constraints and policies of the organization for smooth and continuous operations. Successful socialization accelerates skill acquisition and role mastery, leading to higher productivity. It equips new employees with the necessary knowledge and skills to perform their roles effectively. When new entrants are well-integrated and understand their responsibilities, they can contribute more efficiently to the organization's goals, leading to increased productivity. In an organizational setting, colleagues, superiors, subordinates, clients, and other associates support and guide the individual in learning the new role. Indeed, they help to interpret the events one experiences, such that one can eventually take action in one's altered situation. Ultimately, they provide the individual with a sense of accomplishment and competence.

Apart from role clarity and self-efficacy, which we have discussed earlier, another factor that contributes to high performance is employee accountability. Accountability is about setting clear expectations and holding employees and teams responsible for their decisions, behaviors, and actions in the achievement of common goals (Kolmar, 2021). It is measured by employees' willingness to take responsibility for their decisions, actions, behavior, and performance. That is why key performance indicators are developed for each new employee at the onset, on which they can personally monitor their own performance level. It is during onboarding and socialization that the tasks assigned to new employees are communicated with their expectations and accountabilities. The organization provides a feedback mechanism that highlights progress and areas of improvement, all in the bid to get things done correctly. However, Osemeke (2012) recounts that creating accountability in a very big organization with thousands of employees, with very many tasks and duties, remains a formidable challenge for HR practitioners.

Some practices are encouraged through socialization processes. For instance, creating psychological safety is a fertile ground for new employees to freely participate in decision-making, risk-taking, and sharing of ideas. Also, when onboarding and socialization processes promote cross-functional exposures, this can go a long way to encourage creativity and cognitive diversity, and allow employees to bring unique perspectives. A thoughtfully designed socialization tactic can accelerate role mastery, unlock discretionary effort, and cultivate a climate of high performance. The use of fixed and variable tactics exposes new employees to diverse experiences, often in unpredictable order. This strategy impacts performance in the sense that it encourages consistency and accountability, while the variable impacts innovation through cross-pollination of ideas through varied exposure, problem- solving, agility, and resilience. Similarly, proactive socialization is another tactic that identifies high-potential talents and can positively impact performance and innovation because it enhances engagement and accountability, role innovation and boundary-pushing, as well as fostering psychological ownership and creative confidence. Socialization fosters psychological readiness, cultural alignment, and behavioral consistency, all of which contribute to high performance and innovative capacity. HR leaders can design socialization experiences that unlock both operational excellence and transformative thinking.

Employee Turnover:

Employee turnover involves the consideration of leaving an organization, from the actual leaving. The number of people who quit their jobs or leave an organization within a specific time is referred to as employee turnover, and when calculated as a percentage is called employee turnover rate. Turnover intention is a precursor to the actual turnover and refers to an employee's willingness or intention to voluntarily quit their job or leave a company. The turnover intention is like a warning signal of how many employees are considering leaving the organization. It is a feeling or consideration that, if properly addressed, may not lead to the departure of the employee. Organizational socialization practices are robust means of addressing or lowering employee turnover. New employees who quickly adjust to their roles and responsibilities by understanding what is expected of them, feeling capable of performing their tasks, and fostering effective relationships with colleagues have a strong attachment to the organization, and this bond prevents them from leaving the organization (Guan et al, 2024; Mahmud, 2025). In other words, a well-executed socialization process fosters a sense of belonging and commitment among employees to the point where they become strongly engaged and less prone to turnover.

Employee socialization minimizes turnover rate through several ways, such as psychological adjustment, cultural alignment, job satisfaction, work-life balance, trust, management support, and meaningful connection between the individual and the organization. For instance, during the anticipatory and encounter stages, socialization helps align newcomer expectations with organizational realities. This alignment is important to the point that socialization bridges the gap between what employees expect and what they experience, reducing uncertainty and shock and the likelihood of early exit. It should be noted that misaligned expectations are major causes of disengagement and turnover, and hence, when at the onset, psychological contracts are honored, the new entrants would feel the organization has delivered on its promises. This would not only increase trust and retention rate, but would make new employees feel valued and committed (Gallup, 2018)

Socialization provides employees with role clarity, performance measurement, and success metrics, including self–efficacy (confidence in one's ability to perform). The implication is that employees who understand their role and feel competent are less likely to experience frustration, anxiety, and job dissatisfaction, which are all precursors to turnover. Research has shown that role clarity and self–efficacy are strong predictors of new employee retention within the first six months of their employment (Bauer et al, 2007). In addition, it fosters cultural integration and interpersonal relationships among organizational members, and such interconnectedness makes newcomers feel valued and accepted. On the one hand, social isolation is a key driver of voluntary separation or exit. Furthermore, organizational socialization provides a means through which newcomers internalize the company's values and see their work as meaningful, so that employees who identify with the company and are aligned with its mission are less likely to seek external opportunities. Socialization, therefore, will help to reduce misaligned expectations, lack of support or clarity, and poor cultural fit, which contribute to employee turnover.

Other critical factors that may influence employee turnover include organizational justice, politics, reputation, and communication. Organizational justice refers to how fair and equitable the leaders of an organization are in the allocation of resources, for instance, in employees' salaries and wages, performance evaluation, opportunities for promotion and career growth, etc. It is expected that the management of organizations should be just, unbiased, and transparent in all their dealings, as a lack of justice could demotivate employees, leading to an early exit. One other factor that may affect turnover is organizational politics that brings division among employees, disputes, and internal clashes. Unfortunately, there is no straightforward solution when organizational politics is the main reason for employees' separation from the company. But organizational leaders should show good examples and be sensitive to their actions and behaviors so as to galvanize the support of the workforce towards achieving set objectives. By extension, the company image matters greatly, as employees derive pride in working for organizations with a good reputation. Employees' turnover is likely to be high in companies with a bad image because a company's reputation is associated with the trust and reliability that the stakeholders perceive about it. If a company has a good reputation, it would attract job candidates who want to stay, contribute their quota, and prove their worth. In addition, communication is another factor that can influence employee turnover. According to Jafarzadeh et al (2019), communication is a crucial element in building trust as it is used to convey expectations and clarify accountabilities, and when people know what is expected of them, they are more likely to have confidence in the outcome. A two-way communication gives employees a voice to participate in the decision-making process, buy into the big picture, and feel respected and acknowledged. When employees are kept in the dark and not properly informed about organizational processes, they can become disillusioned and disengaged. This is a turnover intention that must be avoided so that it does not result in actual turnover.

The issue of employee turnover remains a global obstacle for organizations worldwide, which directly and adversely affects strategic plans and opportunities to gain a competitive edge. Since early disengagement often goes unnoticed until resignations begin to occur, HR practitioners should watch out for turnover intentions by employing audit or diagnostic tools to measure socialization effectiveness across units and departments. Regular check-ins and feedback loops allow for timely intervention. There may be a need to conduct surveys while socialization programs are going on to identify at-risk employees and deploy retention strategies before dissatisfaction escalates. It is more proactive to nip turnover intention in the bud because anything done after employees have left is reactive. This will bring immense benefit to the organization; It will save cost in terms of recruitment, preserve institutional knowledge, and stabilize team collaborations and dynamics. No company can progress without the valuable contribution of its members, and so, it is important to keep employees motivated, inspired, and productive.

Organizational commitment:

Organizational commitment has been defined at three levels, namely affective commitment (comprising emotional attachment and identification with the organization), continuance commitment (involving awareness of the cost associated with leaving), and normative commitment (having a sense of obligation to remain). Employee socialization is closely linked with affective commitment, which in turn leads to higher engagement, lower turnover, and stronger performance. This has been defined as the level of enthusiasm employees demonstrate towards the achievement of organizational goals and values. It is the willingness of workers to contribute significant effort for the good of their organization and transcends three levels: commitment to each other's success within the team; commitment to the team's success; and, lastly, commitment to organizational success. As employees bond together, they can surmount challenges and improve performance in tough situations. Organizational commitment is measured on three interrelated dimensions: (a) acceptance of the organization's values (identification), (b) willingness to exert effort on behalf of the organization (involvement), and (c) a desire to remain an employee of the organization (loyalty) (Cook & Wall, 1980; Meyer and Allen, 1991). It is the loyalty, emotional attachment, and willingness to participate in the achievement of team goals, which signifies both the behavioral tendencies and feelings employees have towards an organization (Malik, 2018; Jasmin and Shyni, 2021).

Socialization improves organizational commitment by ensuring identity alignment, interpersonal connection, clarifying roles and responsibilities, and transforming newcomers into loyal, engaged contributors. It also makes the employee buy into the company's vision, refrain from absenteeism, reduces turnover rate, and encourages teamwork in a more immersive manner. In other words, organizational commitment is one of the greatest assets required for organizational efficiency and profitability (Hafiz, 2017).

Employee socialization is linked to organizational commitment in many dimensions. First is through identity affirmation and cultural fitness. Socialization (through investiture tactics) enables new employees to feel seen, valued, and validated for who they are, in such a way that they can express core aspects of their identity (e.g., professional dimension, beliefs, values, gender) without fear or intimidation. Also, it aligns individuals to the prevailing norms, beliefs, and practices of an organization. Together, the two organizational practices predict engagement, reduce identity threats, and enhance value congruence (shared belief about purpose, ethics, and priorities). A properly designed socialization program acknowledges diverse backgrounds, perspectives, and experiences, providing resources, mentorship, and affinity groups that reinforce identity. Obviously, employees who are culturally aligned are more likely to develop affective commitment and integrate with the organization as an extension of themselves. What organizational socialization does is to help employees understand and internalize the organization's values, mission, and behavioral norms.

The second outcome from employee socialization, which has a great influence on organizational commitment, is the fulfillment of the psychological contract. Psychological contract is more of an unwritten set of expectations that defines the relationship of an employee and an organization (employer), which goes beyond a formal employment agreement. It is a reciprocal relationship and obligation in which the employees believe that they own the organization with their effort, loyalty, and discretion; while the organization owes them in return fair treatment, recognition, career development, job security, and good wages, among others (Rousseau, 1995; Ahmad et al, 2019). For example, an employee may expect an increase in wages and career growth in exchange for going far beyond meeting targets (which may not be in a formal contract). If the things expected are met, the psychological contract is fulfilled, and the employee may see it as a breach of contract, which can lead to disillusionment. The theory of psychological contract shows certain key features: it is subjective and implicit in the sense that, unlike formal contracts, it is based on the perception and interpretation of the parties involved. It is not static but dynamic, evolving through interactions and organizational changes. By its multidimensional nature, it encompasses transactional, relational, and ideological elements. The relational are characterized by socio-emotional expectations, in the long-term, whereby the employee believes that in exchange for his loyalty, he would receive career growth or job security. While the transactional features include economic exchange (e.g., pay, benefits) in the short-term, the ideological comprises alignment with values and purpose.

Thirdly, socialization facilitates interpersonal connections through mentorship, peer networks, and team integration. These relationships build trust, psychological safety, and a sense of community and organizational commitment. The effective application of some socialization tactics will enhance loyalty and reduce the desire to seek external opportunities. For instance, serial socialization- involving experienced mentors would deepen emotional bonds; collective socialization fosters camaraderie and shared experiences.

Despite its unwritten and implicit nature, the psychological contract is connected to organizational commitment, engagement, and productivity, and hence HR practitioners should understand this reciprocal deal between employee and the organization and how it can be improved and sustained. Psychological contract fulfillment is a powerful lever for cultivating organizational commitment, and this occurs when employees perceive that the organization has delivered on these implicit promises.

- Fulfillment fosters trust, which is a strong foundation in affective commitment and motivates employees to reciprocate perceived organizational support with loyalty and discretionary effort.
- When ideological contracts are fulfilled, it sends a signal that the organization affirms personal values and identity, emotional investment, and normative commitment.
- Fulfillment of the psychological contract reinforces emotional bonds and perceived moral duty.

The consequences associated with the breach of the psychological contract can be numerous and depend on a variety of factors that would be related to both the organization and the employee, such as characteristics of the labor relationship, the age of the employees, the professional category, and the organizational culture, among other variables. It leads to a lack of organizational commitment, cynicism, and disengagement. Honoring implicit promises has become critical with the modern workforce, given the shifting work norms, heightened expectations, and aspirations. Therefore, to maximize organizational commitment via socialization, HR leaders should consider the following:

- Design socialization programs that encourage the workforce to stay and thrive, and champion the organization's mission.

- Evaluate regularly psychological contract fulfillment through feedback and engagement surveys.
- Ensure mentors are trained to reinforce cultural values and emotional support.
- Use storytelling, rituals, and leadership modeling to reinforce shared purpose.
- Assess the adjustment of new employees in each phase of socialization and, where necessary, correct misplacement early.

References

Ahmad et al. (2019). Do as I say and do as I do?

The mediating role of psychological contract fulfillment in the relationship between ethical leadership and employee extra-role performance. Personnel Review 48: 98–117.

Allen, N. J., & Meyer, J. P. (1990). The measurement and antecedents of affective, continuance, and normative commitment to the organization.

Journal of Occupational Psychology, 63(1), 1–18. https://doi.org/10.1111/j.2044-8325.1990.tb00506.x

Armstrong, M. (2006). Performance management: Key strategies and practical guidelines (3rd Ed.). Kogan Page.

Bandura A. (1977). Self-efficacy: Toward a unifying theory of behavioral change. https://educationalinnovation.sydney.edu.au/news/pdfs/Bandura%201977.pdf

Bauer, T. N., Bodner, T., Erdogan, B., Truxillo, D. M., & Tucker, J. S. (2007). Newcomer adjustment during organizational socialization: A meta-analytic review of antecedents, outcomes, and methods.

Journal of Applied Psychology, 92(3), 707–721. https://doi.org/10.1037/0021-9010.92.3.707

Bauer, T. N., & Erdogan, B. (2011). Organizational socialization: The effective onboarding of new employees. In S. Zedeck (Ed.), APA handbook of industrial and organizational psychology, Vol. 3. Maintaining, expanding, and contracting the organization (pp. 51–64).

American Psychological Association.

https://doi.org/10.1037/12171-002

Bell, T. (2021). Onboarding: Improving Employer and Employee Relations. Applied   Research 2, (1).

https://scholarworks.sfasu.edu/cpmar/vol2/iss1/1

Bhadane et al (2025). On-Boarding process implementation in a global organization: An analytical study. IOSR Journal of Business and Management, 27(1), pp 42-52.

Buchanan, B (1974). Building Organizational Commitment: The Socialization of Managers in Work Organizations. Administrative Science Quarterly, 19(4), pp. 533–546.

https://doi.org/10.2307/2391809

Chao, G. T., O'Leary-Kelly, A. M., Wolf, S., Klein, H. J., & Gardner, P. D. (1994). Organizational socialization: Its content and consequences.

Journal of Applied Psychology, 79(5), 730–743. https://doi.org/10.1037/0021-9010.79.5.730

Cooper-Thomas, H. D., & Anderson, N. (2006). Invited manuscript: Organizational socialization: A new theoretical model and recommendations for future research and HRM practices in organizations.

Journal of Managerial Psychology, 21(5), 492–516. https://doi.org/10.1108/02683940610673997

Deloitte (2023). Fostering engagement, enabling productivity, and reducing turnover.

https://www.deloitte.com/us/en/services/consulting/blogs/human-capital/new-hire-onboarding.html

Didion et al (2024). Mapping the organizational socialization and onboarding literature: A bibliometric analysis of the field.

Cogent Business & Management, 11(1). https://doi.org/10.1080/23311975.2024.2337957

Feldman, D. C. (1981). The multiple socialization of organization members. Academy of Management Review, 6(2), 309–318.

https://doi.org/10.5465/amr.1981.4287818

Frögéli et al (2023). Effectiveness of formal onboarding for facilitating organizational socialization: A systematic review. NLM. 18(2). Doi: 10.1371/journal.pone.0281823.

Gallup (2018). Why the onboarding experience is key for retention.

https://www.gallup.com/workplace/234893/groups-break-company-culture.aspx

Gallup (2021). 8 Practical Tips for Leaders for a Better Onboarding Process.

https://www.gallup.com/workplace/353096/practical-tips-leaders-better-onboarding-process.aspx

Gibbons, M. (2025). Top 8 employee onboarding best practices.

https://peoplemanagingpeople.com/recruitment/employee-onboarding-best-practices/

Guan et al. (2024). Unpacking the effects of socialization programs on newcomer retention: A meta-analytic review of field experiments. Psychological Bulletin.

Advance online publication.

https://doi.org/10.1037/bul0000453

Hafiz, A. Z. (2017). Relationship between organizational commitment and employee's performance evidence from banking sector of Lahore.

Arabian Journal Business Management Review 7(2), 1-7.

https://doi.org/10. 4172/2223-5833.1000304

HBR Survey (2023). A Guide to Onboarding New Hires (For First-Time Managers).

https://hbr.org/2023/07/a-guide-to-onboarding-new-hires-for-first-time-managers

Houle et al (2024). From employee socialization to co-evolution: A lifespan multidisciplinary conceptualization. Applied Psychology.

https://doi.org/10.1111/apps.12572

Jablin, F. M. (1987). Organizational entry, assimilation, and exit. In F. M. Jablin, L. L. Putnam, K. H. Roberts, & L. W. Porter (Eds.), Handbook of organizational communication: An interdisciplinary perspective (pp. 679–740). Sage Publications.

Jasmin, J. and Shyni, K. V. K. (2021). Organizational Socialization as the Key Determinant of Commitment. International Journal of Creative Research Thoughts (IJCRT). 9(12), pp. 842-848.

Jeske, D. & Olson, D. A. (2021). Onboarding new hires: Recognizing mutual learning opportunities.

Journal of Work-Applied Management 14(1):63–76.

Kuusisto, T. (2024). Examining onboarding and employee engagement in field service teams: A case study of Europe and Africa area energy projects.

Kolmar, C. (2021). What is accountability in the workplace?

Zippia.

https://www.zippia.com/advice/what-is-accountability/

Kumar, N., & Pandey, S. (2017). New Employee Onboarding Process in an Organization.

International Journal of Engineering Development and Research, 5(1), 198–206.

https://www.scribd.com/document/488488392/Literature-Review

Ogunbukola, M. (2024). Onboarding is not orientation: Enhancing new hire experiences and retention.

https://www.researchgate.net/publication/378152943

Osemeke, M. (2012). The impact of human resources management practices on organizational performance: A case study of Guinness Nigeria.

An International Journal of Arts and Humanities, 1(1), 79-94.

https://doi.org/10.1016/j.sbspro.2014.11.178

Malik, A. (2018). Strategic performance and commitment management. In Strategic Human Resource Management and Employment Relations (pp. 85-91). Springer.

Mahmud, A. (2025). Exploring the Effects of Employee Socialization.

file:///C:/Users/opara/Downloads/ExploringtheEffectsofEmployeeSocialization.pdf

MATCHR (2025). How onboarding impacts new employee productivity.

https://www.matchr.io/how-onboarding-impacts-new-employee-productivity/

Masoner, L. (2025). The Onboarding process: A step-by-step guide.

https://www.forbes.com/advisor/business/onboarding-process/

Meyer, J. P., & Allen, N. J. (1991). A three-component conceptualization of organizational commitment. Human Resource Management Review, 1(1), 61–89.

https://doi.org/10.1016/1053-4822 (91)90011-Z

Reese, V. (2005). Maximizing your retention and productivity with onboarding. Employment Relations Today, 31(4), 23-29.

Rousseau, D. (1995). Psychological Contracts in Organizations. Understanding Written and Unwritten Agreements. London: Sage.

Salau, O. P., Falola, H. O., & Akinbode, J. O. (2014). Induction and staff attitude towards retention and organizational effectiveness. IOSR Journal of Business and Management, 16(4), 47–52.

https://www.iosrjournals.org/iosr-jbm/papers/Vol16-issue4/Version-6/G016464752.pdf

SHRM (2025) State of the workplace.
https://www.shrm.org/topics-tools/research/2025-shrm-state-of-the-workplace

SHRM (2008). Retaining Talents: A guide to analyzing and managing employee turnover.

https://www.shrm.org/content/dam/en/shrm/topics-tools/news/Retaining-Talent.pdf

SHRM (2022). The real cost of recruitment. https://www.shrm.org/topics-tools/news/talent-acquisition/real-costs-recruitment

Team out (2025). 30 Employee Onboarding Statistics You Must Know in 2025. 30 Employee Onboarding Statistics You Must Know in 2025.

Villanueva, A. (2025). Employee orientation: Definition, importance, and best practices. https://www.outsourceaccelerator.com/articles/employee-orientation/

Wanous, J. P. (1978). Organizational entry: Newcomers moving from outside to inside.

Psychological Bulletin, 84(4), 601–618.

https://doi.org/10.1037/0033-2909.84.4.601

Yu, L. (2020). Three essays on organizational socialization (Doctoral dissertation, University of Wisconsin-Milwaukee). ProQuest Dissertations Publishing.

https://minds.wisconsin.edu/handle/1793/92595

Chapter Five: Employee Engagement

Definitions:

In the last three decades, employee engagement has taken center stage, and hardly is there any popular HR or management publication without the mention of it, and yet there is not one clear and agreed-upon definition as many interest groups describe it in different terms. Hence, the challenge presented by the literature is the lack of a universal definition of employee engagement. However, we attempt to present a few definitions as follows to enable us to have an overview of the concept of employee engagement. According to Khan (1990: 694), employee engagement in terms of psychological state is "the harnessing of organization members' selves to their work roles; in engagement, people employ and express themselves physically, cognitively, and emotionally during role performance." The cognitive aspect of employee engagement concerns employees' beliefs and what they think about the organization, its leaders, and working conditions. Whereas the emotional aspect of employee engagement relates to how employees feel about each of those three factors (their company, supervisors, and working conditions) and whether they have positive or negative attitudes toward the organization and its leaders. Regarding the physical aspect of engagement, this is the physical energy of individuals to accomplish their roles. For

Khan (1990), engagement means being psychologically and physically present when occupying and performing an organizational role.

However, Phifer (2003) sees it as the mental and emotional connection people feel towards the work they do and how they relate to their organization. The mental state is the state of mind whereby members of staff feel a vested interest in an organization's success and are willing and motivated to exceed the job expectations. Whereas the emotional factors tie employees' personal satisfaction, inspiration, and affirmation arising from their work and organization. The emotional aspect demonstrated how people feel about their work experience, in terms of their relationship with the organization, the style of leadership, the work itself, and the work environment. The way and manner people connect to their work and feel committed to the goal of their organization speaks to how engaged they are, as engaged employees will feel excited and enthusiastic about their jobs and will devote extra effort to it (DecisioWise, 2025). Therefore, defining employee engagement will help practitioners understand how individuals interact with the environment, which, of course, is critical to business success, leading to organizational growth and high-performing individuals and teams.

From the above definitions, it is discernible that employee engagement is the level of obligation and involvement employees have in their organizations and their values. Engagement is a positive attitude held by the employee towards the company and its values. That makes it pertinent for organizations to nurture, maintain, and grow their employee engagement, which requires a two-way relationship between the employer and the employee. Most organizations are realizing the fact that a 'satisfied' employee is not necessarily the 'best' in terms of loyalty and productivity. What is required is 'engaged employees who are intellectually and economically bound with the organization; feel intense about its goals and committed towards its values. The challenge today is not only retaining talented people, but also capturing their minds and hands at each stage of their work lives (Kazimoto, 2016). In times of declining loyalty, employee engagement is a potent strategy in driving organizational success. It provides opportunities for employees to align with their managers, employers, and the organization.

The whole essence of employee engagement is to shape an environment where employees are motivated and connected with their job in a real, caring manner, with a view to doing high-quality jobs. Employee engagement practice does not guarantee that all employees in the organization will be equally engaged. There will always be some people who don't want to give their best efforts, no matter how hard HR managers and line managers try to encourage them, but on the other hand, there are others who want to commit themselves to the organization, given the right environment.

Employee engagement is a vital ingredient of individual and organizational success. Engaged employees extend themselves to meet the organization's objectives; take voluntary initiatives; reinforce and support the organization's culture and values; stay focused and vigilant; and believe they can make a positive difference. It has positive linkages to several bottom-line organizational outcomes, for instance, productivity, profits, business growth, product quality, customer satisfaction, employee retention, and job performance (Sundaray, 2011; Dromey, 2014).

When employees are effectively and positively engaged with their organizations, they form an emotional connection with that organization. This impacts their feelings and behaviors toward the company's products/services and customers, thereby increasing customer satisfaction and service levels, and by extension, drives the bottom-line success of the company. High levels of engagement in domestic and global firms promote retention of talents; foster customer loyalty; augment organizational performance and stakeholders' worth. The level of engagement is influenced by many factors such as organizational culture, communication, leadership and managerial styles, and company reputation, among others.

Therefore, the definitions of employee engagement (or characteristics of an engaged employee) revolve around the workforce finding meaning at work, pride, and advocacy of the organization (in terms of advocating /recommending either the products or services of the organization or as a place to work). Another common feature of employee engagement involves workers connecting to the organization's overall strategy and objectives and being able to achieve those (Bhavani et al, 2015: 1-2). Other characteristics of engaged employees include:

- Belief and identification with the organization.
- Going the extra mile and exerting discretionary effort over and above what is normally expected.
- Looks for and is given the opportunity to improve organizational performance.
- Keeps up-to-date development in his/her field.
- Treats others with respect, helps colleagues perform more effectively.
- Sees the bigger picture, even at personal cost.

Evolution of the concept of employee engagement:

There was no mention of employee engagement in the early 20th century (1900s-1930s) of the industrial age and scientific management. The focus then was on productivity, efficiency, and standardization, and employees were seen as tools of production. However, between the 1940s and 1970s, there was an emphasis on employee well-being and motivation, and they were greatly influenced by Elton Mayo (Hawthorne studies), Abraham Maslow (Hierarchy of Needs), Douglas McGregor (Theory X and Y), and Fredrick Herzberg (Two-factor theory), amongst others. Within this period, the use of both intrinsic and extrinsic motivation was widely used as a means of sustaining employee satisfaction. The period was replete with lots of studies measuring job satisfaction and morale, and their correlation with performance. This is what laid the foundation for what would later become employee engagement.

Moving forward, a lot of developments have taken place around employee engagement between the 1980s and 2000s. Companies began to realize that job satisfaction and employee morale were not sufficient for organizational performance, commitment, and innovation. There was a quest for a more dynamic psychological connection between employees and their work, and concepts like organizational citizenship behavior, employee empowerment, job enrichment, job autonomy, and quality of work life (QWL) began to gain traction. The earliest forms of employee engagement were studied under terms like employee participation, involvement, commitment, or morale. It is important to mention the contributions of William Kahn (1990), who popularized the concept and was a pioneer scholar, often credited as the father of employee engagement, who linked engagement to the discretionary effort of employees who are willing to go the extra mile. In his work titled "Psychological Conditions of Personal Engagement and Disengagement at Work," published in the Academy of Management Journal, he identified three psychological conditions for engagement, namely, meaningfulness (does the work matter?); psychological safety (can I express myself without fear?); and psychological availability (am I mentally and emotionally present?). Other organizations that played a significant role in the growth of employee engagement include, but are not limited to, Gallup, Aon Hewitt, Towers Watson, among others. For instance, Gallup developed surveys in the early 1990s and started studying the correlation between employee engagement and performance outcomes. Companies like IBM and General Electric began to recognize that engaged employees are necessary for their innovation and competitive advantage.

As a result of the immense impact employee engagement had on organizational success, HR consultancy firms began to work with organizations to develop metrics to quantify employee attitudes and behaviors as well as their impact on customer satisfaction and organizational performance. Most references to the evolution and development of employee engagement tend to relate to survey houses and consulting firms. It is less taken as an academic construct. Studies undertaken by Rafferty et al (2005) indicate that it originated from consultancies and survey houses rather than from academia. The level of interest it has generated indicates that it is more than a passing management fad, and a considerable amount of research and analysis has been conducted in the last 10 years or so, building up our understanding of the term.

Also, as globalization and the sophistication of technologies continue to evolve, they pose more challenges for managers because organizations will need a greater number of employees with increased technical and professional skills. These knowledge workers need to be properly managed and engaged. Hence, the attention of managers is shifting towards the employees' side of organizations. Moreso, the millennials (those born from 1981-1996) and Gen Z (those born from 1997-2012) are reshaping the landscape of employee engagement in terms of their expectations towards purpose-driven work, flexibility, and meaningful impact. This is because they come new worldview that is technologically driven, a desire for meaningful work, and global mindedness. Since these generations of workers constitute a large number of the workforce and come with their unique values, expectations, and behaviors, employers are forced to redefine their strategies of keeping these categories of workers fully engaged to gain a competitive advantage. In many organizations, this has led to the redesign of their communication channels, management styles (adopting coaching and mentoring approaches), and workplace design (providing hybrid and flexible work systems and workplace culture that promotes inclusion, transparency, and social responsibility. The rise of the knowledge economy was an indication that intellectual capital and discretionary efforts are important business differentiators.

Between 2000s-2020s, many organizations have integrated employee engagement into HR strategies and employee engagement and are using it to measure business outcomes, such as profitability, turnover, and productivity. To this end, it has become normal for organizations to conduct annual engagement surveys, and the emergence of the employee value proposition has become part of talent strategy. As businesses are striving to increase their performance, managers have been grappling with many challenges to succeed in putting their company ahead of competitors, and one of the strategies that comes in handy is employee engagement. Higher employee engagement levels tend to reduce absence and turnover levels, while eliciting positive employee attitudes, higher productivity, quality customer experience, loyalty, high shareholder returns, and better financial performance. It can transcend into many tangible and intangible benefits for organizations. This is because engaged employees are emotionally attached to their organizations and are highly involved in their jobs with greater enthusiasm for the success of their employer, going an extra mile beyond the employment contractual agreement. For these reasons, employee engagement is a hot theme, and organizations are using different engagement-building tools to remain competitive and improve performance. In fact, employee engagement is now recognized as a key driver for organizational success and a critical factor for organizations to gain a competitive advantage.

In today's world, what makes one company more successful than another is not only better products, services, strategies, technologies, and better cost structure; they all contribute to superior performance, but all of them can be copied over time. One of the factors that creates a sustainable competitive edge is a competent workforce that is fully engaged. They outperform work groups that are not engaged. In the fight for competitive advantage, where employees are the differentiator, engaged employees are the goal. There is a consensus that efficiency and productivity lie within the employees' ability and commitment. Managers' eyes are on how to keep employees engaged in their jobs. Employers have now realized that by focusing on employee engagement, they can create a more efficient and productive workforce. Any initiatives of improvement that are taken by management cannot be fruitful without the willful involvement and engagement of employees (Markos and Sridevi, 2010). Employee engagement has become a very important managerial construct and has been absorbed into the human resource (HR) agenda. It is a vast area of study that touches almost all parts of human resource management facets we know, and if every part of HR is not addressed in an appropriate manner, employees will not be fully engaged in their job roles. The topic is capturing the attention of executives, professionals, and academicians.

Figure 1.2: Summary of the Evolution of Employee Engagement:

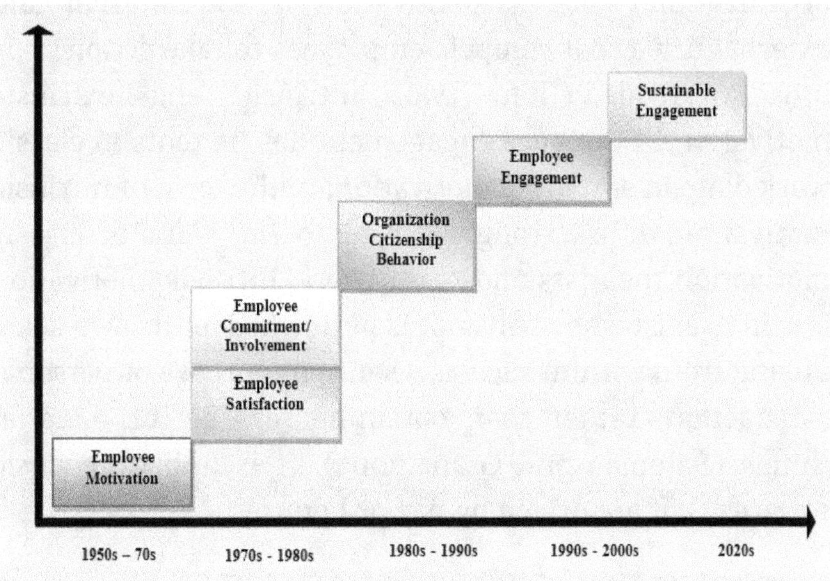

Terms used interchangeably with employee engagement:

Employee engagement is built on the foundation of earlier concepts like employee satisfaction, employee commitment/involvement, and Organizational Citizenship Behavior (OCB). Though these terms predate employee engagement, they are similar in many ways and can be seen below:

Employee engagement versus motivation:

Though the two terms are related and sometimes used interchangeably, they are not the same in meaning, application, and impact. Employee engagement describes the commitment people have towards their jobs and the organization. Whereas motivation is the internal and external drive that compels employees to take action. It is broadly divided into two: intrinsic and extrinsic motivations. Employee engagement has its roots in classic work done in employee motivation, in the form of intrinsic motivation. It is strongly linked to the work of classic motivation theorists and researchers. Intrinsic motivation is said to exist when behavior is performed for its own sake, arising from within, such as a sense of purpose or personal satisfaction, rather than obtaining tangible or material things (Bateman and Grant 2003). It is unlike extrinsic rewards that are driven by pay or bonuses.

The difference between employee engagement and motivation is that while the former drives action, the latter fosters commitment. For example, a motivated person may perform well in the short run, but an engaged individual will sustain superior performance. The similarity is that a motivated individual can become engaged when their roles align with their values and when they feel supported or recognized. Also, an engaged person is likely to be motivated to give high performance because of his/her emotional connection to the organization and the work.

Employee engagement versus employee satisfaction:

Satisfaction is an integral part of employee engagement. While they are related, the difference is that employee engagement is the emotional commitment one has to an organization and its goals, which keeps them/ motivated and willing to go the extra mile. But employee satisfaction describes the degree to which an employee is content with his/her job and working conditions, such as compensation. It is transactional and provides employees with basic compensation, tools, resources, and physical safety-factors which do not motivate, but their absence can lead to demotivation of employees. However, engagement is transformational, using the heart, spirit, hand, and mind to give employees a peak experience that makes them eager to give extra discretionary effort. Employees may be satisfied with their job, show up every day, but not necessarily engaged. They may stay with the company but will not perform optimally and may even resist change. For example, a satisfied employee may like job security and pay, and do what is required and no more. On the other hand, an engaged employee is one who is emotionally invested and, for this reason, goes far beyond devising means of improving performance, helping colleagues to achieve goals, and staying late at work to resolve customers' issues. Employee Satisfaction is a weaker predictor and lacks the two-way reciprocal relationship characteristic of engagement.

Employee engagement versus commitment/ involvement:

Employee commitment is the degree to which employees identify themselves with an organization. Allen and Meyer (1090) define the three types of commitment as follows:

- Affective commitment: describes the emotional attachment of employees towards an organization.
- Continuance commitment is the perceived recognition of the cost of leaving an organization, and normative commitment is the moral obligation to remain with an organization.

In comparison, the closest to employee engagement is affective commitment, which explains the level of enthusiasm employees demonstrate towards the achievement of organizational goals and values. This type of commitment can be measured at three levels: (a) employee acceptance of the organization's value (identification), (b) employee willingness to exert effort on behalf of the organization (involvement), and (c) employees' desire to remain with the organization (loyalty) (Cook and Wall, 1980). Affective commitment is associated with the willingness of employees to contribute significant effort for the good of the organization, and Malik (2018) asserts that this is a result of employees' loyalty and emotional attachment to an organization. On the other hand, employee engagement is about how employees perform in terms of their passion, enthusiasm, and willingness to exert energy. Both overlap, indicating reasons why high-performing companies employ the two concepts in creating a workplace where people love their work and where they work.

Organizational citizenship behavior (OCB):

Employee engagement and OGB are similar and hence are used interchangeably. It is defined as discretionary and voluntary behaviors exercised by employees that are not formally rewarded, even though they contribute positively to the realization of organizational goals. These behaviors include:

- Helping colleagues who have fallen behind in their work (altruism).
- Showing initiative beyond job requirements (conscientiousness); demonstrating performance over and above what is expected.
- Tolerating inconvenience without complaining (sportsmanship); being able to carry on with a positive attitude in the face of adversity, and being willing to set aside personal interests for the good of the organization.
- Having macro-level interest in the organization, such as a loyal citizen would display towards their country (civic), promoting the organization to the outside world, and staying committed to it, even when doing so could involve a personal sacrifice.
- Preventing work-related conflicts (courtesy).
- Voluntarily improving one's own knowledge, skills, and abilities in such a way as to be helpful to the organization (self-development).

The above highlights characteristics of OCB and largely resonates with employee engagement- a psychological state that involves vigor, dedication, and absorption, which is a reflection of the employees' emotional, physical, and cognitive investment in the actualization of organizational goals. Employee engagement is manifested when workers demonstrate high levels of energy and mental resilience to their work, strong involvement in their duties, and are concentrated or engrossed in their work. By implication, engaged employees are most likely to exhibit the characteristics of OGB.

Although the behaviors associated with the engaged employee have much in common with those demonstrated by the good organizational citizen, OCB is concerned with the characteristics and behavior of the individual, rather than the organization. Another distinction is on the basis that engagement is a two-way mutual process between the employee and the organization. In engagement, there must be a mutual feeling of support between the employee and the organization. Employee engagement also differs from Organizational Citizenship Behavior (OCB), as engagement is concerned with the passion (psychological investment) for one's role, while OCB is concerned with extra-role and voluntary behavior, which is largely attitudinal. Furthermore, while engagement constitutes an internal state that informs how employees perform their duties, OGB is an external manifestation of behaviors beyond formal job requirements.

The future and the sustainability of employee engagement:

As the world of work evolves, employee engagement continues to be of important consideration. We are in a rapidly changing global landscape, and for this reason, the future of employee engagement is being redefined to meet expectations around emerging technologies, the workforce, and the inclusive workplace. The strategic nature of employee engagement has placed it on a continuous journey characterized by adaptability, empathy, and increased focus on well- being and purpose. Organizations that want to embrace the future are rigging their engagement strategies to boost performance and innovation and to become an employer of choice in an increasingly competitive business landscape. This has not been easy to achieve for some organizations due to the challenging economic climate. Business concerns are now more than ever deciding to restructure and resize, which has resulted in organizations investigating new approaches to maintain and increase engagement. Many companies have shut down, and the signal to workers is that 'there is no job for life', and to survive in this terrain, workers are acquiring new skills and moving to where the job can be found. Employers soon realized that they were losing people they did not want to lose. It was costing them money and affecting their ability to compete effectively. The current challenge for employers up till today is how to get employees fully engaged for a competitive edge and to sustain business success.

HR departments are making efforts to recruit, train, and motivate their talent, with a view to retaining their best. Firms are striking the right balance between fostering and enhancing employee engagement levels while at the same time not compromising their competitive position. As employee engagement progresses in the future, it will not be a strategy that is owned by HR alone, but something that needs to be owned and driven by the CEOs and the entire leadership team of organizations. For employee engagement to be sustainable and effective, it needs to be owned by everybody, including the employees. Engagement measures should be aligned to managers' performance through KPIs- Key Performance Indicators. (HRZONE, 2013).

The future of engagement is more about sustaining it rather than finding the next hot HR theory about how to attract, motivate, and retain good employees. As demographics change, different generations of workers are found in the workplace and predominantly dominated by the millennials (1981-1996), generation Z (1997-1912), and lately generation alpha (2013 to date) with their differing expectations. Some employees now seek a short-term career as a stepping stone, with the expectation of moving from jobs that are less satisfying to better jobs. On the other hand, organizations want employees to put extra effort and generate innovative ideas to save money and improve services. It is an engagement that will give organizations the tools to provide the kind of workplace that will attract, retain, and motivate their changing workforce. Engagement has reached the point in its growth where it requires clarity and consistency of definition, delivery, and measurement. There are very few businesses that are against employee engagement; the problem is more about doing something about it, particularly those in the Small and Medium Enterprise (SME) sectors, which don't have the same resources and infrastructure as larger organizations (HRZONE, 2013; Macleod and Clarke, 2012).

The COVID-19 pandemic brought a trajectory to the world of work as companies went through lockdowns, remote work, economic disruptions, and health crises, which accelerated hybrid work. In the post-pandemic era, this work model has become the norm, and companies that want to be rigid or resist this shift will continue to lose their valuable talents. As we move further into the post-pandemic era, employee engagement will comprise emotional connection, purpose, flexibility, psychological safety, and well-being, which need to be deployed in a sustainable manner, not only to retain talent but to spark off innovation, high performance, and long-term success. Also, employers should be looking forward to creating outcome-based performance metrics, rather than results based on hours worked, while establishing connections with employees through virtual check-ins, engagement surveys, and AI-driven employee insights. Organizations in the future should be open to flexibility in how, when, and where the work should be carried out. Undeniably, the future of employee engagement is also interwoven with AI-powered solutions. Using technology as a double-edged sword plays a vital role and can create an agile, resilient, and employee-centric workplace. It provides the advantage of offering real-time insights into employee sentiments and makes way for more personalized engagement strategies. Leaders must be able to find ways of encouraging workers to embrace technology, and it is safer to highlight that AI is not replacing people with their jobs, but it is aimed at empowering businesses and making the workers more productive. Despite the huge benefits, overreliance on digital tools can lead to fatigue, depersonalization, and erosion of workplace relationships. Attention should be focused on creating a human-centered environment to ensure connectivity, rather than isolation.

The future of employee engagement is an evolving one that will be characterized by a value-driven culture, and this will compel companies to articulate and live out their authentic values, whereby employees will feel their work contributes to the big picture. Also, the quality of leadership and management style will continue to take center stage, and sustainable engagement would mean that organizations should have leaders and managers who listen actively, are emotionally intelligent, skillful in managing hybrid teams, and willing to empower employees with autonomy and growth opportunities. Employee engagement will continue to thrive through integrated strategies that are focused on enhancing employee well-being, inclusive culture, trust, transparency, and above all, creating meaningful employee experiences that match their individual aspiration and needs.

Drivers of employee engagement:

Many researchers have tried to identify factors leading to employee engagement and to draw implications for managers. Their aim is to determine the drivers that will increase employee engagement levels. Most drivers that are found to lead to employee engagement are non- financial in nature. This does not mean that managers should ignore the financial aspect of their employees. Highlighting the factors that enable engaged behaviors is almost as tricky as identifying a single concrete definition of employee engagement. Employee engagement is driven by many antecedents, and a few are presented as follows:

Work environment and culture:

The physical and psychological conditions under which employees perform their duties refer to the work environment and may include workplace design, tools, and technologies. Organizational culture relates to shared values, beliefs, norms, and practices that govern behavior in the workplace. The work environment addresses the tangible, and organizational culture deals with the intangibles that define social interaction and psychological safety. Both work environment and culture shape the way workers perceive their roles and responsibilities, relate with others, and align with the company's vision (Judeh, 2021).

One of the important issues to consider in the work environment is job design. According to Torrington et al. (2011), this is "the process of putting together a range of tasks, duties, and responsibilities to create a composite for individuals to undertake in their work and to regard as their own" (p.84). Basically, job design is an attempt to improve the efficiency of the business as well as improve employee satisfaction. It is also a deliberate attempt to structure both technical and social aspects of the job with a view to achieving a fit between the individual (job holder) and the job itself. The underlying principle is the fact that employees need to have control over the aspects of their work, enhance the quality of their lives, and harness their potential in a more effective manner to improve performance. As a matter of fact, it takes care of the capabilities and needs of those who are to perform the job. It must include factors that satisfy employees' personal growth needs and provide a feeling of responsibility, meaningfulness, and knowledge of results. The way an organization chooses to construct its jobs can affect the attitude and behavior of its employees. If it is properly designed, it will impact on the motivation, performance, and job satisfaction of those who perform them. Unfortunately, job design remains a topic that receives much less attention from some employers and policymakers as a major driver of employee recruitment and engagement compared with other aspects of management, such as leadership or management style (Truss, 2012). There is a dearth of information available for employers on the key principles of job design and the major factors that need to be taken into consideration when designing engaging jobs. Some studies have found a correlation between work environment and employee engagement (Sak, 2007; Anitha, 2014; Judeh, 2021).

Designing jobs that promote employee engagement would require consideration of some factors, such as the organizational, environmental, and behavioral components of the workplace. The organizational factors would include:

- Task Features: This consists of a group of defined tasks or activities to be carried out. Good job design should involve several tasks to be performed by a group of employees. For example, each task should have these internal features: planning, execution, and control. Also, the task must incorporate a maximum degree of intrinsic motivation for those who will carry it out by improving the quality of working life.
- Workflow: Every job that needs to be done has to be sequenced so that it can flow in relation to other jobs, in the most efficient and effective manner. For example, in a furniture company, making a table and a chair will involve sourcing the right wood, cutting it into shapes, joining them together, and polishing or decorating. What it means is that the sequence of tasks is

determined to make a workflow.

- Ergonomics: This is the term used to describe the study of the physical arrangement of the workspace, together with the tools used to perform a task. In ergonomics, we strive to fit the work to the human being rather than forcing the human being to conform to work. The job is designed not to harm the jobholders. The principle is that workers should adopt several different postures that are safe and comfortable. Also, ergonomics ensures that jobs are designed to enable the utilization of the workers' physical, mental, and emotional abilities to perform effectively.
- Work Practice: This refers to standards or a set of ways of doing work based on tradition or the collective wishes of employees. Work practices should be taken into consideration in Job design. The consequences may be great if they are ignored.
- On the other hand, the environmental factors would consider issues like:
- Social and Cultural Expectations: Jobs need to be designed to meet social and cultural expectations. Globalization has brought about an increase in awareness. The level of literacy, education, and knowledge has equally increased. These reflect on the type of job people choose. Therefore, in design, careful consideration must be taken in features like work hours, restrooms, break-time, dressing code, vacations, etc. Ignoring these social/cultural expectations can create dissatisfaction, low motivation, high turnover, and low quality of working life.
- Employee Ability: Due consideration should be given to employees' ability when affecting job design and

redesign. This is in order not to create a mismatch between the job and the job holder.

While the behavioral factors need to be given adequate attention. Much of what we know today about job content design emanates from the seminal work of Hackman and Oldham (1980), who developed the job characteristics model. This identifies five core motivational job features: a variety of skills, autonomy, responsibility, significance, and feedback, which managers can leverage to enhance employee engagement:

- Variety of Jobs/Skills: Job design should incorporate elements of variety in the jobs. This will help minimize boredom and fatigue. It should also encourage employees to use a vast range of skills.
- Autonomy, Responsibility, and Challenge: The employee wants the freedom to control his/her actions/responses in the work environment. Autonomy increases the sense of responsibility and self–esteem among workers, whereas the absence of autonomy brings about workers' apathy, low morale, and poor performance. Therefore, a job should be designed in such a way that each employee has responsibility, challenge, freedom, and the opportunity to be creative. Delegation can be a powerful tool for improving a job. It is likely to have positive impacts on employees. People whose work is autonomous experience a feeling of responsibility and are then more likely to invest effort into their work, even in the face of obstacles (Shantz et al., 2013).
- Significance: Job or task significance refers to the degree

to which the job significantly impacts the lives of others both within and outside the workplace. Job designs should consider the importance of each job, and the job holder should also understand the significance of his/her job to the organization and outside the organization.

- Use of Abilities: Most of the employees will prefer jobs that offer them opportunities to make use of their competencies. They will find it interesting and challenging.
- Feedback: It is necessary to provide feedback on the job design. Well-designed jobs anticipate the need for communication. Most employees want to know what is expected of them and how they are faring in their jobs, too. They want to know so many things, such as: how they can improve, what should be discussed with the supervisor, and when the discussion should occur. Employees rarely complain about too much communication, but they can complain about a lack of communication. Suffice it to say that meaningful feedback can help workers improve their performance.

According to Hackman and Oldham (1980), jobs with high levels of the above-listed features are the most motivational. The reason for this is that these job characteristics give rise to the following psychological state:

- Experienced meaningfulness or the ability to see your work as meaningful in some way.
- Experienced responsibility or feeling responsible for the outcomes of your work.

- Knowledge of results, or the ability to see the outcome or the impact of your work.

In addition, jobs with these characteristics are most likely to lead to high levels of performance, positive attitudes towards work, and decreased negative attitudes and behaviors. The reason why Hackman and Oldham's job design features are important for engagement can be understood within the context of psychological theory. For example, people whose jobs are varied are more likely to experience a sense of energy in relation to their work (Engage for Success, 2014: 4). Parker et al (2001) extend Hackman and Oldham's original model by proposing additional characteristics relevant to modern management, thus:

- Opportunity for skill acquisition, growth, and development, especially transferable skills.
- Minimization of role conflict, which is important particularly for front-line workers who often must play multiple roles.
- Cognitive Characteristics: It has been predicted that increased attention and increased problem-solving are required.
- Emotional Characteristics: Work in the modern era increasingly demands emotional labor, for example, service work.

The need for a work environment that would keep workers fully engaged has led to the deployment of some techniques that are commonly used today, and some of them are highlighted below:

- Job Simplification: Another name for job simplification is "job specialization". This is the breaking down of work into small sub- parts and then analyzing them. Each sub-part (small part) is assigned to an employee, who does it over time to acquire proficiency or specialization. Specialization has two parts to job design. On the one hand, it promotes high-speed, low-cost production and can greatly enhance the standard of living. On the other extreme side, workers can experience boredom, frustration, alienation, lack of motivation, and low job satisfaction.
- Job Enlargement: According to Nicholas (1982:532), the job enlargement strategy is an "attempt to increase satisfaction and performance by consolidating work functions from a 'horizontal slice' of the work unit to provide greater variety and a sense of the whole task". Job enlargement refers to increasing the number and variety of tasks within a job. For example, a marketer can wait on customers, finalize sales, help with credit applications, arrange merchandise, and render stocks. With this number of assignments, it can be said that he has an enlarged job. A job is said to be enlarged horizontally if a worker performs a greater number or variety of tasks, and when it is enlarged vertically, it means that the worker is involved in planning, organizing, and monitoring of his/her own work. Horizontal job enlargement is intended to counteract over- simplification or specialization. It is to enable a worker to perform a whole unit of work. Vertical enlargement (traditionally termed job enrichment)

attempts to broaden workers' influence in the transformation process by giving them certain managerial powers over their own activities.

- Job Enrichment: This is an approach in job design that emphasizes that employees can be motivated by satisfying their survival needs and then adding motivation to create job satisfaction. It may add additional responsibilities or tasks that provide more variety and autonomy to a given job. It involves varying some aspects of them to increase the potential to motivate employees. Sometimes employees want more from their jobs than is now possible. Job enrichment is a response to employees' readiness for more responsibilities, variety, and challenge. According to Luthans (2008), job enrichment is concerned with designing jobs that include a greater variety of work content, require a higher level of knowledge and skill, give workers more autonomy and responsibility in terms of planning, directing, and controlling their own performances, and provide the opportunity for personal growth and meaningful work experience. Some of the job dimensions that contribute to enrichment and consequently lead to employee engagement include direct feedback- providing employees with performance reports and how to improve performance. Secondly, the provision of personal accountability and control. For instance, delegation of responsibility, authority, and control is a key feature of job enrichment, which empowers employees to have control over work methods, resources, and work schedules. Thirdly, it affords workers a unique experience to undertake challenging jobs that would elicit their creativity and innovation.

- Job Rotation: This refers to the movement of staff from one job to another. The employees perform different jobs, but of the same nature. Job rotation is the temporary switching of job assignments. It helps employees to develop job-related skills. In the process of job rotation, employees learn how other units and departments function. The issue of repetitiveness that causes frustration, boredom, and injury may be reduced. However, too frequent job rotation is not advisable in view of its negative impacts on the organization and the employees. Employees may feel alienated as they move too frequently from one job to another, especially when they move from a more challenging job to a less challenging one; frustration may set in.
- Work Scheduling: This is another aspect of job design. In recent times, scheduling of working hours is receiving attention against the traditional 5 working days per week, eight hours per day, and 40 hours per week, which is the standard for most of the country's labor force. The work schedule, therefore, is a formal departure from the traditional hours of work. It is aimed at improving performance as well as employee satisfaction. A variety of work scheduling targeted at balancing family needs, personal needs, and organizational needs is highlighted below:
- Compressed Workweek: A compressed workweek is a full-time schedule that allows employees to work 40 hours in fewer than five days. What it means is that the employee may work for three or four days to cover the forty-hour work week. The organization can benefit from it in terms of reduced absenteeism, improved

recruitment of new employees, and having extra time available for building and equipment maintenance. It is liked by employees whose lifestyle fits into such a schedule. However, many employees do not have the energy to work the prolonged hours required in the compressed workweek. It is also incompatible with the operation of some works.

- Job Sharing: Another aspect of job scheduling is job sharing. It involves two or more people sharing a single job. The most common practice of job sharing is a full-time job being converted into two part-time positions. The two part-timers agree with the employer to divide the job, and the compensation is attached to it. The job can be shared on a daily, weekly, or monthly basis.

- Part-time and Temporary Work: Part-time and temporary work is very prominent in the UK and the USA, as about two-thirds of employers use this aspect of work schedule. It appeals to employees who choose to reduce their working hours to create more time for their personal lives. Part-time and temporary work provide benefits to both the employer and employees. It allows for greater flexibility in the work schedule, and it provides a balance between the employees and the work. It is a cost-saving strategy as part-time and temporary work rarely receives statutory benefits. The labor union often kicks against this kind of work schedule because it reduces the job opportunities available to its members.

- Flexible Working Hours (flextime): This means the work has flexible beginning and ending times. Flextime usually eliminates common beginning and ending times for employees doing the same job. Rather, the employer permits the workers to choose daily starting and quitting times. However, employees with flexible working hours are needed at certain core hours but have flexibility in starting and ending times.

- Telecommuting: This is an arrangement in which employees use computers to perform their jobs at home or in a satellite office. The advancement in technology has led to the relocation of work from the office to the home. It is beneficial because it makes life easier for employees and helps employers improve productivity. Overhead costs, such as renting and furnishing large office spaces, are minimized. It attracts talented staff and makes recruitment easier. There are some shortcomings with telecommuting in the sense that managers may find it difficult to coordinate work done at different locations. There may be some jobs that require face-to-face contact to get clarification. Some other disadvantages include career retardation, workaholism, and procrastination. Loyalty and teamwork may be difficult to develop.

Organizational culture:

Organizational culture can be described as the personality of the organization. Organizational culture has been defined as "a pattern of shared basic assumptions that the group learned as it solved its problems of external adaptation and internal integration that has worked well enough to be considered valid and, therefore, to be taught to new members as the correct way to perceive, think, and feel in relation to those problems." (Schein, p.18). This definition asserts that organizational culture is a deep-seated assumption, often learned and passed on, and usually guides perception and behavior. Similarly, Scholz (1987) views organizational culture as "the pattern of basic assumptions, values, norms, and artefacts shared by members of an organization, which defines appropriate attitudes and behaviors for members and shapes the way the organization conducts its business." In other words, organizational culture comprises visible and invisible elements (artefacts and assumptions; it shapes behavior, and above all, it is shared among members of the organization. Organizational culture, though powerful and multifaceted, is a major driver of employee engagement, especially when it aligns with employee values and enhances trust, growth, and is authentically lived by leaders. Cultures that recognize and promote innovation, effective internal communication, and reputation and integrity are key to setting the tone of engagement (Bui & Le, 2023; Ravi, 2023). Similarly, organizations that are considered 'employer of choice' are more likely to have higher levels of employee engagement. This is because they create a work environment in which employees feel respected and valued, recognized and rewarded, and with systems of work–life balance, where workers would be receiving help from their employers to achieve a good work– life balance (Glen, 2006, and Lloyd Morgan, 2004). How many employees are prepared to endorse the products and services that their company provides to its customers depends largely on the image of the company and their perceptions of the quality of those goods and services. High levels of employee engagement are inextricably linked with high levels of customer engagement.

One of the areas in which organizational culture can promote employee engagement is value alignment. Value alignment is the extent to which individual and team values resonate with those of the organization. When personal and organizational goals are congruent, certainly, employees are more likely to experience a sense of belonging, purpose, and motivation, all of which are essential components of engagement. The essence of value alignment is to ensure that individual objectives align with organizational objectives, and it does this by establishing a high-performance culture in which individuals and teams take responsibility for the continuous improvement of business processes and for their own skills and contributions. Any strategic alignment will link the organization's goals with individual goals and reinforce behaviors that are consistent with the attainment of organizational goals. Even if for some reasons individual goals are not achieved, linking individuals with organizational goals serves to communicate what the most crucial business strategic initiatives are (Kristof-Brown et al, 2025). It also helps in making individuals more engaged in goal attainment.

Value alignment creates an environment where people feel emotionally connected, motivated, and committed to the vision of an organization. It is in the process of aligning values that organizations not only enhance employee satisfaction and performance but also cultivate a resilient and purpose-driven workforce. When there is compatibility between individual values and the core values espoused by the organization, this will, in turn, promote a sense of belonging, purpose, and motivation. Value alignment has been examined by Kristof-Brown et al. (2005), and according to the authors, person- organization fit can significantly affect job satisfaction, commitment, and retention, especially when they believe that their ethical values, work ethic, and goals align with their employer's vision, mission and culture, they tend to be more intrinsically motivated and committed to achieving high performance. For example, an employee who values diversity, equity, and inclusion (DEI) works for an organization that actively promotes DEI; he is most likely to feel proud and energized. This alignment fosters an emotional bond that goes beyond extrinsic and transactional employment and taps into the intrinsic and psychological contract between employee and employer.

Today, many organizations have developed organizational strategies that emphasize the "person-organization" fit as a means of sustainable success. It is easy for leaders to assume that everyone knows and understands what the organization is for and what it is trying to achieve. But vision, strategy, and a sense of purpose need to be clearly articulated and communicated so that employees in all areas of the business develop a shared understanding of organizational aims and objectives and understand how their job role fits in with and contributes to them. Everyone needs to be able to look beyond their day-to-day work and get the 'big picture' of what is happening across the organization and where the organization is heading in the future. It can be a powerful tool for improving the business's performance. Connecting individuals to business goals and strategy is a powerful driver of engagement.

Another factor organizational culture highlights revolves around making the work meaningful and purposeful, which is a critical antecedent of engagement. Rosso et al. (2010) describe meaningful work as "work experienced as particularly significant and holding more positive meaning for individuals." What it means is that the work must be perceived as significant to the job holder, contributing to the employee's sense of identity and aligning with the intrinsic values of the organization. Purposeful work is related to meaningful work and describes job roles that contribute to a broader mission or social impact beyond personal gain. In other words, it connects one's personal contribution to an organization's big picture or global outcomes. Meaningful and purposeful work is about the employee's perception that his/her job is important and has a clear purpose and meaning in the organizational priorities. For example, employees need to feel that the work they are doing is important, not only for themselves but for the organization, to the extent that they have a sense of pride that their contribution is helping their company to make a difference in the marketplace. Therefore, making a difference toward a cause can offer a sense of fulfillment to employees. On the other hand, this has significant implications for job designs to ensure that the meaning and purpose of the job roles are clearly defined. By designing jobs that promote employee engagement, organizations create jobs where workers will be challenged and stimulated, have authority and autonomy, access to information and resources, and growth and development opportunities (Gema and Carl, 2009).

Though meaningful and purposeful work is a human motivator, it behooves organizations to clearly articulate their vision and mission and show how employees' efforts contribute to the broader goals. There is a need for modern business concerns to provide meaningful and purposeful work that will not only provide employees with opportunities for growth but will also retain, engage, and inspire the workforce. Hence, leaders must be at the center of it all by instilling a culture where meaning and purpose thrive and help employees find meaning by validating what they bring to the table and aligning them to the organizational vision. Leaders will reinforce a sense of meaning and purpose when they act with integrity, communicate openly, and acknowledge how the employees' work contributes to the realization of the organizational mandate. Also, recruiting people whose personal values are in tandem with organizational values ensures a better person– organization fit. Learning and development programs should reinforce these values to build a consistent culture.

One other dimension of organizational culture is trust and psychological safety. Pauline et al (2010) define trust as the confidence or belief a person feels toward a particular individual. Employee engagement is essentially relationships based on trust, especially in times of uncertainty, and hence, Frei and Morris (2020) are of the view that the absence of trust brings fear, anxiety, confusion, and inaction. No doubt, trust is the foundation of every human relationship and creates the conditions for employees to fully maximize their potential and power. It fosters collaboration and minimizes interpersonal conflict. For instance, if team members trust one another, they can share responsibilities and help each other complete their tasks on time and align with organizational goals. People trust organizational leaders who are authentic, transparent, and empathetic in their relationships. It is important for employees to know that their leaders are not just focused on their own personal agendas but have the interests of the whole organization and its workforce at heart. To earn the trust and loyalty of their employees, leaders and managers must be visible and authentic. They must be seen to speak the truth and act with integrity. If there is a statement of organizational values, leaders should model those values in their own behavior.

Trust in leadership begins to manifest when employees feel inspired by their top leadership, coupled with actions leading to business success. Building trust is necessary to help organizations drive performance, but this can only happen when expectations are clearly defined and managed. It is on this background that Gallup (2023) highlights what the best leaders do to earn the trust of their subordinates, and this would involve:

- Communicating Clearly: Trusted leaders provide a clear vision for their people, and this entails what is going on and how people should do their work. When leaders clearly couch their vision and the approach needed to achieve it, they provide their employees with a road map for where to focus their energy.
- Inspiring Confidence: Followers do not need to have every detail of the plan, but a broad sense of the primary goal. It is the duty of the leader to give information in digestible chunks, instilling confidence in the people about the strategic direction and letting subordinates understand the step-by-step actions of how to achieve the plan or the big picture.
- Leading and Supporting Change: When leaders support change, employees are more likely to believe in them, especially when they show how the change will positively affect the employees and the organization. This involves a two-way communication that makes employees believe in their leadership.
- Listening to Employees: There is no doubt that all businesses run on communication. When employees feel that they have the opportunity to provide honest

feedback about innovation and organizational changes, they are likely to have confidence in their leaders to manage the change process, including the challenges thereof.

Gallup (2023) concludes that leaders can improve the level of trust in an organization by exhibiting authenticity (a practice developed consciously and consistently), transparency, and leading with the competencies that inspire trust. Authentic leaders are those who lead with integrity, self-awareness, and a deep commitment to their values. They're not just skilled managers; they're people who inspire trust by being genuine and consistent. Authenticity makes the leader's intentions and ethics predictable, which makes it easier for employees to feel confident in and trust their leaders. Transparency is sharing that truth through words, behaviors, and actions. Ultimately, transparency is fundamental to trust, but transparency is only effective when properly transmitted. In addition, leaders who commit to certain leadership behaviors or competencies can inspire trust in individuals. These competencies include the ability to build relationships, focusing on followers' needs, expectations, and aspirations; the capacity to inspire others; communication skills; the need for accountability; and critical thinking.

On the other hand, Kahn (1990) identifies psychological safety as a vital condition for engagement, which enables individuals to express themselves without fear of negative consequences to self-image, status, or career. Psychological safety is the belief that employees are safe for interpersonal risk-taking and, as a result, can express themselves, admit their shortcomings, and challenge the status quo without fear of punishment. Both psychological safety and trust foster a high level of employee engagement. Generally, employees engage in work situations they perceive as safe, trustworthy, predictable, and clear in terms of behavioral consequences. Safety is largely promoted by the quality of relationships with colleagues and managers, which need to be open, trusting, and supportive. Engagement levels can be low if the employees do not feel secure while at work, hence, every organization should adopt appropriate methods and systems for the psychological and environmental safety of their employees (Vazirani, 2006:7). While trust is more interpersonal and anchored around relationships, psychological safety is a team dynamic, involving many employees who perceive their environment as safe or not. The role of trust and psychological safety is crucial in employee engagement, especially in this era of constant organizational change, increasing complexity, and workforce diversity. Both concepts are interrelated and underpin how employees perceive their environment, relate to their leaders and peers, and decide whether to bring their full selves to work.

Furthermore, leadership styles and internal communication are deeply rooted in organizational culture.

Leadership plays a key role in shaping the work environment and culture that enhances employee engagement. When leaders set a clear and compelling vision, they can influence employees to buy into that vision, leading to a shared vision. Shared vision generates commitment within an organizational context. Johnson et al (2019) define vision as the big picture of the organization and what they stands for. It is the duty of leaders to articulate the vision and strategies and, in turn, communicate it to all employees to develop a shared understanding of organizational aims and objectives and, by extension, how their role fits into the big picture. In their research, Martin et al (2014) have shown that "vision helped leaders and their teams to become inspired and committed to a shared goal ...provides orientation and meaning for leaders and their team" (p.1). It is a strong force for employee engagement and collaboration (Phillips and Juster, 2014). In organizations where managers and leaders give employees the opportunity to participate in decision-making, they will feel valued and respected, and will feel engaged and motivated to go the extra mile. It is, therefore, the responsibility of organizational leaders to make their employees feel that the core values for which their company stands are unambiguous and clear; show respect to each employee's qualities and contribution, regardless of their job level, and create ethical standards that lead to engagement of employees. The leaders of high-engagement workplaces create a trusting and challenging environment in which employees are encouraged to dissent from the prevailing orthodoxy and to input and innovate to move the organization forward. Employees want to be involved in decisions that affect their work.

While leadership sets the tone, communication provides the mechanism that brings the intention of leadership to life, and without it, the most inspiring leadership may not succeed in engaging employees. Employee engagement is driven by opportunities for upwards feedback, effective consultation and communication systems, and a manager who is fair and visibly committed to the organization. A whole range of different methods is used by organizations to keep their employees informed and up to date. These include meetings, briefings, newsletters, and corporate intranets. When it comes to engagement, what matters is not the methods used but the effectiveness, regularity, and consistency of the communication put in place. It should also be open and honest, focusing on positive progress and achievements as well as the challenges and difficulties faced by the organization. No one likes to feel that they are being kept in the dark or being given a false impression of the true situation. This undermines confidence and trust in leaders and can lead to disillusionment and disengagement. Communication should be two-way, i.e., between the employer/manager and the employees. Organizations should have channels through which communication is enhanced within, where they interact with their employees, helping them feel valued and respected, and so that their expectations and aspirations are taken seriously.

Employees need to know that their views and opinions will be heard and taken into account, and that they can safely raise issues that concern them. It is particularly important for senior managers to be visible and approachable. Some organizations provide email access to senior management so that employees can ask questions or put forward ideas.

Together, leadership and communication are two intertwined elements that form the bedrock of where employees feel valued and motivated. Leadership provides direction, trust, empowerment, and recognition, while communication helps these attributes to be effectively conveyed and reinforced. The best leaders create an environment where employees feel safe and prioritize open, honest, and empathetic communication as an integral part of their leadership practice.

Connecting employees to business strategy:

Given today's dynamic workplace, it has become necessary to align employees with business strategy and, by extension, have them understand what the organization is for and what it is trying to achieve. For this reason, the vision, strategy, and a sense of purpose need to be clearly articulated and communicated so that employees in all areas of the business develop a shared understanding of organizational aims and objectives and understand how their job role fits in with and contributes to them. Everyone needs to be able to look beyond their day-to-day work and get the 'big picture' of what is happening across the organization and where the organization is heading in the future. It can be a powerful tool for improving the business's performance. Connecting individuals to business goals and strategy is a powerful driver of engagement because when individual members of the organization understand how their work supports the big picture, their roles take on a renewed sense of purpose and meaning. This connection transforms their day-to-day duties into great contributions, thereby empowering them to see their impact beyond their immediate responsibilities. The fact is that when everyone is connected to the business strategy, it creates an engagement culture where people engage, evolve, and excel. In a nutshell, aligning employees to business strategy comes with numerous benefits, such as:

- Boasting Motivation and Ownership– this reinforces employees' ego, respect, and a sense of inclusion and belongingness.
- Enhancing Performance and Accountability– properly defining tasks and objectives goes a long way in helping align employees' efforts to organizational priorities and how to measure success against benchmarks. It builds a culture of accountability where individuals understand what peak performance looks like.
- Strengthening Collaboration– employees are not only connected to company priorities but to other individuals and teams within the organization, towards common outcomes.
- Encouraging Continuous Learning– employees can identify their skill gaps (where they need to develop),

and the organization can support their learning efforts.

Recognition, appreciation, and rewards: Recognition, appreciation, and rewards are strategic levers that shape organizational culture and deepen commitment as well as employee engagement. While recognition and appreciation focus on acknowledging and valuing workers' contributions, rewards can serve as an additional layer of motivation, often in tangible forms, for positive behavior and performance. Properly designed recognition, appreciation, and reward systems could support employees' sense of internal motivation, satisfaction, and engagement (SHRM, 2024; Forker, 2025).

Recognition speaks of the basic human need, where individuals want to feel accepted and acknowledged, particularly for their contribution within a team or an organization. The affirmation sends a strong signal of employees' presence and output, creating the awareness that they are not just filling a seat but are making a meaningful impact. Also, recognition opens the channel of honest and constructive communication. It is obvious that when leaders and managers take time to recognize the good work of their employees, it conveys a sense of care and attention; and employees reciprocate this gesture by trusting their leaders and contributing their ideas, and stretching themselves beyond their comfort zones. Furthermore, recognition helps employees take initiative and contribute innovative ideas, knowing that their efforts will be noticed and valued.

Similarly, appreciation acts as a powerful reinforcement mechanism for employee engagement. No doubt, when an employee's specific actions or behaviors are praised, those actions are likely to be repeated and create an atmosphere where individuals are inspired to give their best consistently. It must be noted that appreciation goes beyond acknowledgement to nurture emotional well-being. As engagement is tied to emotional connection, employees who feel emotionally supported are more likely to be productive and exhibit organizational citizenship.

Apart from feeling recognized and appreciated, employees need to be rewarded, and meaningfully, too. It must be rewards that align with employees' personal and professional goals. Such rewards may be in the form of opportunities for learning and development, flexible working hours, and extra time off. Companies should have a proper pay system so that the employees are motivated to work in the organization.

Receiving timely recognition and rewards is a key driver of engagement. The degree of formality of such recognition is determined by circumstances and what is appropriate. Employees need to feel valued and appreciated for the work they do. Organizations may need to consider the needs and motivations of different groups of employees–older workers, younger workers, or disabled workers by providing a cafeteria of benefits. (Lockwood, 2007; Blessing White, 2007).

Three elements are crucial in making appreciation, recognition, and reward as drivers of employee engagement. Providing recognition that builds on the following areas can improve employees' engagement, satisfaction, and long-term outcomes:

- Addressing Strategic Goals: Recognition and rewards must be able to reinforce desirable behaviors and align individual efforts with the company's goals.
- Meaningfulness: Recognition that offers social approval and signals career value, reinforcing the significance of one's work.
- Security: Positive reinforcement contributes to psychological safety and trust in the workplace.
- Self-efficacy: Genuine acknowledgment builds employee confidence, encouraging continued high performance.
- Care of Employees: When leaders show that they care about their subordinates' personal and professional journeys, it reinforces the connection between employees and their organization.

Learning and development opportunities:

As the workplace evolves, having access to learning and development opportunities is considered a driver of employee engagement. This is because when they feel they are growing intellectually, professionally, and career-wise, they are more productive, motivated, and committed to their work.

Opportunities in learning and development send a signal that an organization is invested in its people. It is common knowledge that for employees to perform well, they need to have the right skills for the job, and their roles need to encompass work that the employee knows how to do, but with scope to learn new skills and develop their role. When companies initiate plans around career management, succession planning, mentoring, and other developmental efforts for their employees, they are simply looking forward to engaging their employees. Organizations with high levels of engagement provide employees with opportunities to develop their abilities, learn new skills, acquire new knowledge, and realize their potential. On a broader scale, it has gone beyond skill acquisition to enhance employee engagement, retention, and overall organizational success. Kumar (2024) asserts that employees with access to learning and development opportunities are significantly more engaged, up to 3.5 times when compared to their peers without access to learning opportunities.

- In today's workplace, there are diverse learning styles aimed at meeting employees' career aspirations, and we will attempt to highlight a few below:
- Personalized Learning: A one-size-fits-all learning and development is becoming a thing of the past; hence, organizations are creating training to match individual learning styles, preferences, and career goals. Personalized learning has become popular because employees are seeking to meet their unique needs that

align with their career goals, and they do this by choosing their own training paths, which provide them with a sense of autonomy. This strategic approach enhances engagement and makes employees feel valued.

- Digital Learning Experiences: This is intertwined with employee engagement, especially in the modern workplace that is technologically driven. Digital platforms enable employees to learn at their own pace (microlearning), thereby creating a sense of ownership and intrinsic motivation, which is crucial for engagement. Microlearning allows employees to engage in focused, brief learning sessions that fit seamlessly into their daily routines, promoting continuous learning without disrupting workflow. Using digital platforms, learning is made available to everyone, and this helps to promote equity and a sense of belonging. It makes learning not only interesting but interactive; by incorporating gamification, simulations, and multimedia content, these formats help employees retain whatever they have learned and, at the same time, stay emotionally invested in their development. Most importantly, since learning is tailored to reinforce the organization's strategic value and priorities, the alignment exposes employees to have an understanding of how their roles prove to be of help to the bigger picture.
- A Culture of Continuous Learning: Kumar (2024) highlights that 45% of employees are more likely to stay longer with companies that prioritize continuous L&D initiatives. For this reason, employee engagement thrives in learning organizations, where the

organizational culture requires concerted effort to prioritize learning. To engage employees effectively, learning programs must include continuous learning across the organization, and every employee is encouraged to seek growth opportunities, learn from colleagues, and stay curious. The outcome would be that learning is prioritized and integrated into the organizational culture, so that people feel more connected with their roles and the organization itself.

- Prioritizing DEI in Learning: Incorporating diversity, equity, and inclusion into learning programs is one way of building inclusiveness at the workplace. The implication is that it will help to eliminate unconscious bias and promote cultural competency. When employees feel that their identities are recognized and respected, they have a sense of belonging and tend to be more engaged and satisfied. Hence, DEI learning programs would foster an inclusive culture, which in turn would significantly increase engagement and loyalty in a diversified work environment.

- Coaching and Mentoring: These are developmental tools, but beyond that, they are also powerful employee engagement drivers. Coaching and mentoring are used to build trust and mutual respect, and the coach or mentor leverages the process to make the employee feel supported, share ideas, and deeply engage with their work. By doing so, coaching and mentoring provide psychological safety, which is a strong element of employee engagement. In addition, it supports the emotional resilience and well-being of employees, which helps them navigate challenges, build confidence, and manage stress. As employees benefit from coaching and mentoring, they not only gain fresh perspectives but also show up with purpose, passion, and pride. These practices transform employee experience and elevate their engagement with the organization to the extent that they become more invested in their roles as well as the future of the company.

- Future Trends: As the workplace evolves, learning and development will still focus on individualized growth, employee well-being, and inclusive culture. Emphasis will continue to be placed on creating a workplace where employees feel inspired, safe, motivated, and supported to achieve the organizational mandate.

When organizations invest in the learning and development of their people, they reap the benefits of a higher level of engagement. Through training and development, employees will feel confident in their abilities to perform in their roles. This confidence, in turn, leads to greater engagement and motivation to succeed. Also, it increases job satisfaction as employees is given opportunities to learn new skills and develop existing ones, which is demonstrated in stronger commitment to the organization. Furthermore, it enhances employee loyalty and a culture of continuous learning.

Work-life integration:

Work-life integration evolved from work-life balance and emphasizes the integration of professional and personal responsibilities, finding harmony and ensuring that they complement each other. It is unlike the traditional concept of work-life balance that keeps work and life separate. Work-life integration acknowledges that people do not stop going to school or taking care of their children because they are working. It has become an important driver of employee engagement in the sense that it allows both life and work to coexist. Some of the characteristics are that employees have flexibility over rigidity- for example, Employees are at liberty to choose when they perform their tasks rather than drawing lines between personal and work time. It is difficult to differentiate home and work as employees may choose to work from the bedroom or kitchen. Secondly, success is measured by results, not by hours spent at a desk. Thirdly, digital platforms allow people to work from anywhere, making it easier to integrate work into daily life, and lastly, individuals can choose when they're most productive, whether that's early morning, late evening, or in bursts throughout the day.

According to Wooll (2022), the benefits of work-life integration are as follows:

- Employees can give equitable attention to all aspects of their lives without sacrificing one for the other, thereby enhancing their well-being, mental health, and engagement at the workplace.
- It is very realistic and practical; for example, employees can stay connected and collaborative, even when working from home, and leaders can follow work

processes in real-time.

- It utilizes technology to streamline tasks and improve efficiency. As employees feel empowered when in control of their work and time, this in turn elevates their confidence and self-esteem. It is not rigid but flexible. For example, encouraging employees to choose their most produce it prioritizes tasks based on urgency and importance to enhance productivity.
- It reduces the stress of trying to separate professional and personal life, which can be overwhelming, in such a way that both are handled without any encroachment on the other.

In today's fast-paced world, the concept of work-life integration offers a fluid and flexible approach to balancing professional and personal lives (Samtharam & Baskaran, 2023). Work-life integration is no longer a trend, but a response to the changing face of today's interconnected world. The concept has come to stay because it acknowledges that people can still be parents, caregivers, students, and at the same time pursue their career lives; so that by allowing life and work to coexist, an individual can live a fulfilled life in terms of well- being, productivity, and engagement.

Benefits and Outcomes of Employee Engagement:

An organization's capacity to manage employee engagement is closely related to its ability to achieve high performance levels and superior business results. Companies with engaged employees enjoy higher employee retention because of reduced staff turnover, lower absenteeism, and thus are able to capitalize on the savings associated with attrition. Higher engagement levels are also associated with sharp increases in productivity, customer satisfaction, and performance indicators, leading to discernible elevation in the overall profitability levels of the firm (Macey et al., 2009; Harter et al, 2013; Abdou, 2024; Vintage Circle, 2025). Some of the advantages (outcomes) of engaged employees are:

Customer loyalty/employee advocacy:

Engaged employees play an integral role in enhancing customer experience levels, reputations, and bottom lines of businesses. Customers are more likely to recommend a business to others if they have had a positive experience, and that positive experience is most often formed by interactions with the frontline staff of the organization. The way customers are handled by the employees of the organization plays an important role in them forming a perception about the image of the organization and deciding their loyalty towards it. According to Levinson (2007a), "in departments where highly engaged employees sell to engage customers, customer loyalty, repeat purchases, and recommendations to friends are double that of companies with average employee engagement." Ultimately, this may lead to what is sometimes termed 'customer engagement', where there is a mental and emotional connection between the organization and the customers (Bates, 2004). Clearly, engaged employees understand the value of ensuring a positive customer experience and are more likely to demonstrate their commitment by delivering high-quality products and services.

When employees are engaged, there is a tendency for them to become advocates and ambassadors for their organization through word-of-mouth. They develop emotional attachment and a sense of pride and talk about their company with enthusiasm. Employees' word- of - mouth is very powerful because it is believed to come from people with first-hand knowledge of the company and its products or services. The positive outcome is that they help to promote their company's brand in a competitive market. As employees become advocates of the company, they also attract more customers, leading to customer loyalty.

While most disengaged employees would actively discourage friends from joining their current organization, engaged employees can extend their advocacy to recommending the organization to potential job seekers as a place to work and employer of choice, thereby reducing recruitment costs. They are willing to do free marketing aimed at enhancing the public image of their organization. To make employees well-positioned to become their company's strong ambassadors will entail the following:

- Creating a positive organizational work culture where people are physically and emotionally connected with their organization.

- Creating a work environment where the vision is not only clear but shared among employees.
- Creating a workforce that is recognized, motivated, and rewarded.
- Creating a transparent workplace, and workers have a voice.

Employee retention:

The economic turbulence over recent years has had an unsettling impact on many employees who have chosen to switch jobs in search of organizations aligned with their personal goals, providing career certainty and financial security. According to Blessing White (2008), about 85 percent of engaged employees would stick around an organization compared to 27 percent of disengaged employees. In addition, 41 per cent of engaged employees said that they would stay if the organization were struggling to survive. Engagement and retention have thus become firmly rooted in current talent management strategies and practices, viewing employees as strategic assets that are a fundamental precondition to achieving improved business results through effective human resource engagement. Effective engagement of employees can reduce intention to leave, lower annual turnover, and greatly lessen the costs associated with attrition, thereby ensuring huge savings for the organization (Ahlowalia et al, 2004: 314). They would prefer to stay and grow within the company instead of searching for new opportunities. Besides the actual monetary cost of turnover, increased employee retention translates into reduced disruption and more stability.

Employee productivity:

Employees who are more engaged at their workplace are more efficient and productive because they are motivated beyond personal factors (Kazimoto, 2016). Engaged employees, without a doubt, are more focused and more motivated than their disengaged counterparts. This means they work more efficiently and keep the success of the organization in mind. When employees are connected to their organizations and feel valued, they take pride in their work and are more likely to go above and beyond what is expected. This is because they understand the big picture and want to do their best to contribute to it. The efforts exerted not only boost individual performance but also elevate team dynamics, leading to increased productivity, sales, and revenue. They can do so because they are proactive in identifying areas and processes that can be optimized. Productivity increases because employees take ownership of their work, seek to reduce waste, and eliminate bottlenecks that hinder operational efficiency. There is no doubt that engaged employees find their work meaningful and will make an effort to increase productivity. On the other hand, a disengaged employee may feel miserable and stressed out and may not give their best in terms of performance.

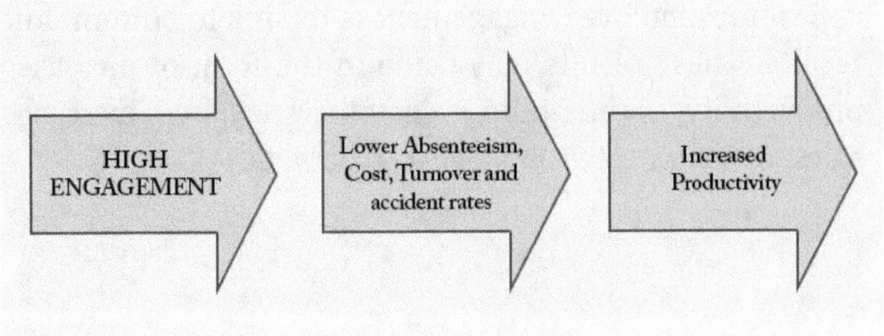

Figure 1.3: High employee engagement leads to increased productivity:

Increase Revenue and Profitability:

Employee engagement has a positive impact on key business metrics, leading to better organizational performance and efficacy. Engaged employees directly influence the bottom line and outperform disengaged employees in revenue growth, profitability, and long-term sustainability. The reason is clear: they take initiatives, solve problems proactively, and complete projects on time with fewer errors and use resources more efficiently. The simple logic is that when operational efficiency improves, cost decreases, leading to higher profitability. Other factors that bring about increased revenue and profitability include innovation and creativity; improving customer satisfaction; reduced turnover and talent cost; and strategic alignment and goal achievement- all are fueled by employee engagement. Organizations that prioritize employee engagement would create better business outcomes. People Management (2008) concludes that the appeal for employee engagement is its link to bottom-line results. These results may come in the form of increased productivity, profitability, customer loyalty, increased sales, or better retention levels (Dajani, 2015).

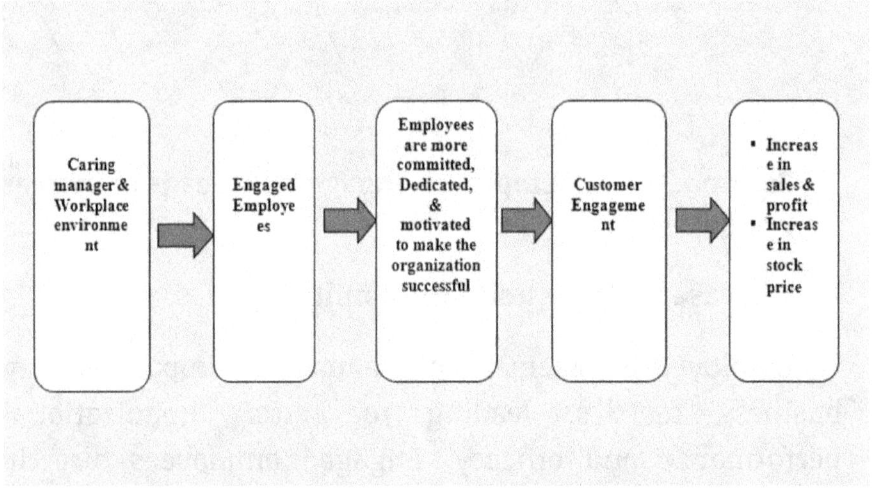

Figure 1.4: High employee engagement leads to increased revenue and profitability.

Improved employee wellbeing and health:

One of the benefits of employee engagement is the huge impact it has on employee wellbeing, improving work–life balance and work–life integration, and reducing the risk of burnout, exhaustion, cognitive and emotional impairment. This is possible because engaged employees feel a strong sense of control and purpose at work and hence can handle pressure and manage their workload more efficiently. Also, the sense of feeling valued, cared for, and supported helps them mitigate stress-related issues. Investment in employee engagement programs that promote well-being and work-life balance can reduce absenteeism. Given the fact that people have limited time, energy, and bandwidth, it becomes necessary to balance professional and personal life to enhance mental and physical health. It allows people to recharge and re-engage with their duties with renewed enthusiasm and focus. To maximize employee well-being and health, it is advisable that organizations take measures like providing mental health resources, workplace safety, work-life integration, time off and leave policies, and wellness programs.

Intrinsically motivated:

Employee engagement is a gateway to intrinsic motivation. Intrinsic motivation is the internal drive that propels individuals to work for the satisfaction and joy that the work brings. Unlike extrinsic motivation, like salary and bonuses, it is deeply personal and enduring. One of the ways to encourage this kind of motivation is through employee engagement, where people are emotionally connected to their work and the work aligns with their values, and inspires them to contribute meaningfully. Organizations looking forward to cultivating intrinsic motivation through employee engagement should consider the following:

- Creating a sense of purpose and meaning: This is the foundation of intrinsic motivation, when employees understand the vision and mission, and how their work

contributes to the big picture.
- Provide employees with opportunities to learn and grow: When employees feel they have learning opportunities that provide them with growth and improvement, they experience a deep sense of satisfaction, which in turn drives them to continue investing in their work.
- Promoting autonomy and ownership: Employee engagement empowers people to embark on projects, make decisions, and take ownership, thus fueling intrinsic motivation.
- Fostering connection and belongingness: employee engagement helps workers feel valued, respected, and connected to colleagues and leaders. This relationship creates a sense of belonging and enhances intrinsic motivation.
- Promoting flexible work arrangements.
- Encouraging teamwork and collaboration.
- Offering constructive feedback.
- Celebrating small wins.

Boosting Leadership Development:

Employee engagement creates fertile ground for leadership development by promoting trust, ownership, and a culture of continuous learning. Engaged employees are more motivated to undertake leadership roles, and the dedication and commitment they exhibit make them ideal leaders within the organization. Organizations that prioritize employee engagement would naturally raise leaders who can take initiatives and solve problems; they go beyond managing tasks to inspire teams and drive change. Leadership development programs thrive in workplaces where the employees are engaged. Several reasons account for this, including the creation of an environment of psychological safety and open communication; the emphasis on empathy, active listening, trust– building, and constructive feedback, which accelerates their development into emotionally intelligent leaders. Leadership development programs flourish in environments where individuals are encouraged to stretch beyond their comfort zones and embrace growth in areas like coaching, mentoring, and skill–building initiatives. These skills are crucial in setting clarity around roles, expectations, and performance goals. Hence, organizations that invest in employee engagement are directly investing in authentic and impactful future leaders.

Strengthening workforce flexibility:

Employee engagement fosters workforce flexibility because when employees are happy and satisfied at work, they are willing to adapt to changing scenarios at the workplace. Organizations are increasingly saddled with changes that would require the workforce to be flexible if the evolving needs are to be met. Employee engagement prepares people to be more adaptable, responsible, and committed to making flexible work possible and productive. This is on account of the symbiotic relationship between employee engagement and flexible working conditions, as each reinforces the other to create a thriving, resilient workplace. For example, engagement enhances emotional connection to work, while flexibility supports work-life integration, and both help to reduce burnout and improve employee well-being. Employees who feel supported in their professional and personal lives are more loyal, motivated, and flexible. Employees' flexibility is reflected in their ability to embrace new technologies, strategies, and processes to improve their contributions. One of the factors of employee engagement that helps in strengthening workforce flexibility is trust. This trust is important for flexible work arrangements, such as virtual work or flexible hours, where supervision is minimal. Flexible work arrangements, when supported with engagement, can lead to job satisfaction and superior performance; energizing employees to deliver results, knowing they are trusted and valued.

Promotes diversity, equity, and inclusion (DEI):

DEI is intertwined with employee engagement, and organizations that embrace both practices create a thriving and equitable workplace. Employee engagement is rooted in emotional connection and a sense of purpose, where people from all backgrounds feel valued, respected, and empowered. An inclusive culture and perspectives are one effective way to advance DEI through employee engagement. When DEI is part of the core value of an organization, it opens the door for diverse people who bring their full selves to work, thereby enhancing creativity, problem- solving, and innovation. When organizations align DEI with engagement strategies in such a way as to encourage inclusive leadership, personalized paths, transparent promotion, and reward systems, they inspire employees to grow. They also become open to collaborating with employees from within and outside the department, sharing knowledge and achieving common targets.

Employee Engagement Strategies:

Companies that prioritize engagement do so for many reasons, not only to foster employee retention and productivity, but also to cultivate a culture where individuals bring in their best. To enshrine such a culture, organizations must adopt a multiple approach that reflects every aspect of the employee experience, from the first day at work to the point of exit, on issues such as leadership, communication, well-being, etc. A solid culture of employee engagement does not just happen; it is purposefully planned and carefully implemented to cure what Kular (2008) describes as employee disengagement disease. The step-by-step approaches to building employee engagement in an organization are as follows:

Make a business case:

Without a business case, it may prove to be difficult to convince business leaders of the need to invest in employee engagement. Employee engagement requires leadership commitment through establishing a clear mission, vision, and values. Unless the people at the top buy into it, own it, and pass it down, employee engagement will never be more than just a "corporate fad" or "another HR thing". When employees understand the mission and values of their organization, they are more likely to feel connected to their work. Employee engagement does not need lip service, but rather a dedicated heart and action-oriented service from top management. It requires leading by example, and leadership must actively champion engagement by modelling transparency, empathy, and support. Hence, the business case should be able to highlight the benefits of the engagement by identifying the strategic goals and how to achieve them. These organization-specific benefits make the vision and potential of an engaged workforce feel "real" for the organization. It is the duty of the leaders and managers to serve as a bridge between organizational goals and individual aspirations. Basically, the first stage will require clear identification of what engagement means to your organization; the measurable goals you want to achieve (e.g., customer satisfaction to be increased by 20%; reduce employee turnover by 10%); and aligning the business case to the big picture of the organization. All these provide a roadmap for decision-making and help to measure progress over time.

Assess current engagement levels:

Before embarking on an engagement program, it is crucial to understand the current state of engagement. This would entail gathering data through employee surveys, exit interviews, performance metrics, and focus groups. The areas to pay attention to would be around job satisfaction, burnout risk, workplace relationships, trust in leadership, emotional well-being, work-life integration, etc. This diagnostic phase helps identify strengths to build on and pain points to address. Creating opportunities for employees to offer feedback and contribute ideas would uncover what would get an employee to stay at the company and any causes of disengagement.

Design engagement strategy:

Having obtained data from the employee survey, the next step is to design a strategy, and this should be multifaceted, involving initiatives like:

- Recognition programs: Celebrating the team's hard work and contributions in meaningful ways can positively impact engagement, not only for the employees being recognized but also for those witnessing the act of recognition. Many organizations use the system of rewards to incentivize and acknowledge contributions, such as hitting sales targets, completing projects ahead of schedule, and suggesting innovative ideas, which all attract points.
- Professional development: providing training, mentoring, and career growth encourages engagement and proves to employees that an organization is invested in their career progress, making it more likely for them to reciprocate such gestures by committing their best to the organization.
- Wellness initiatives: supporting mental, physical, and emotional health helps in promoting engagement. Adding wellbeing programs like on-site fitness centers,

financial counselling, and mental health resources is vital in enhancing engagement levels, because when thoughtfully implemented can reduce burnout risk significantly.

- Flexible work arrangement: Empowering employees with autonomy and work–life balance is vital when building employee engagement. Granting employees control over their work processes and environment lets them work in ways that best suit their productivity. Similarly, policies that support employees' flexible work schedules, personal time off, and family commitments are more likely to enhance engagement.

Communicate the plan transparently:

Managers should promote two-way communication that allows employees to ask questions, share feedback, and feel involved in shaping the culture. This is the bridge between strategy and execution. What needs to be communicated is the purpose, benefits, and expectations of the engagement plan. Transparency builds trust and encourages buy-in and creates a culture of inclusion, reducing uncertainty and aligning teams with shared goals. Employees are not sets of pots to which you pour out your ideas, without giving them a chance to have a say on issues that matter to their jobs and lives. Clear and consistent communication of what is expected of them paves the way for an engaged workforce (Balakrishnan and Masthan, 2013). Involve your people and always show respect for their input. Share power with your employees through participative decision- making so that they would feel a sense of belonging, thereby increasing their engagement in realizing it. The employer must listen to their employees and remember that this is a continuous process. The information employee's supply will provide direction. This is the only way to identify their specific concerns. When leaders listen, employees respond by becoming more engaged. This results in increased productivity and employee retention. Engaged employees are much more likely to be satisfied in their positions, remain with the company, be promoted, and strive for higher levels of performance. To encourage communication within an organization, the following may be helpful:

- Creating multiple channels of communication that connect with peers, managers, and top leadership.
- Creating channels of communication that convey each employee's responsibilities and performance expectations, and how they are to be measured.
- Build in one-on-one check-ins with their direct reports to share and receive feedback.
- Create an open-door policy that makes leadership more accessible to every employee.

Implement engagement initiatives:

Having laid the groundwork, it is time to implement the strategy in phases, starting with high-impact initiatives. Managers play a vital role in engagement programs because of their working relationship with employees. As frontline ambassadors, line managers are expected to treat employees as individuals, with fairness and respect, and show concern for the well-being of employees. Leading with empathy, providing regular feedback, and supporting team development are essential at this stage. Also, technology can be used to ensure that all employees have access to engagement initiatives.

Monitor progress and collect feedback:

Employee engagement is not static but an ongoing journey. It should be measured at regular intervals to track its contribution to the success of the organization, through surveys and performance metrics, to enable leaders to identify areas of improvement. Conducting regular survey of employee engagement level brings to light, factors that are promoting engagement; and at the end of each survey, it is advisable to sum these factors into two or three areas and begin actions on the factors that will make the most difference to the employees- putting energy and improving these areas may be a good approach, as it may be difficult to address all factors at once. It is important to continuously refine engagement strategies based on data gathered and adapt to changing needs to sustain long-term engagement. It is always good to know what is working and what is not.

Celebrating engagement wins:

There should be time set aside to celebrate milestones, share some success stories, and acknowledge progress already made. Recognizing engagement wins publicly has a way of boosting morale, reinforcing positive contributions, and motivating employees to get involved in engagement efforts. This can be done in many ways, such as:

- Highlight and celebrate individual/team achievements in company- wide meetings.
- Celebrate and share stories of engagement success in newsletters/intranet.
- Recognize individual/team outstanding contributions with badges or perks.
- Encourage peer-to-peer contribution for engagement-related actions.

As mentioned earlier, employee engagement is a continuous exercise, and therefore, for organizations to remain agile and relevant, there would be a need to refine engagement strategies based on feedback and evolving needs.

Employee Engagement Measurement:

Measuring employee engagement is among the best organizational practices because a business is as successful as its employees. Tracking engagement helps HR understand and influence key outcomes, like productivity, innovation, retention, and customer satisfaction. Disengaged employees hurt morale, slow down progress, and are more likely to quit. Measuring engagement early helps fix problems before they worsen. It also strengthens HR's role in long-term planning by demonstrating to leadership the connection between employee engagement and business performance. Regular feedback and action based on data can also build trust among employees, as it shows them that their input matters. However, for employee engagement to be properly measured, one needs to be aware of the challenges in the process.

One of the challenges to bear in mind is that engagement is emotional and subjective, and difficult to measure using employee engagement metrics. Sometimes the measurement indices are too broad, infrequent, and not honest, hence leading to misleading results. To minimize the weakness, it is advisable to use both quantitative and qualitative surveys, the former being less detailed because results are based on numerical responses. While quantitative methods collect and measure numerical data, qualitative methods take care of the intangible aspects of the data that are still of great value in the research process. Remember that employee engagement can be difficult to measure because it is inherently intangible. Therefore, without reading your employees minds, it is difficult to know how they really feel. That is why we apply flexibility–instead of measuring engagement directly, we try to identify key metrics that give us insight into employee engagement levels. Ideally, the use of interviews and focus groups would help a great deal in understanding current sentiment and engagement levels. Some organizations may organize small group sessions or focus groups where managers work closely with employees to drill down into issues uncovered by engagement surveys. These are usually conducted through guided discussions on topics and by inviting employees to share their thoughts. It could also take the shape of a one- on-one meeting between managers and employees, and this may serve as a regular touchstone for managers to evaluate employee engagement, as well as assist team members in overcoming any difficulties they are facing.

It must be noted that employee engagement. Does not have to be a task performed solely through surveys. This can be measured by looking at the key performance indicators (KPIs) to assess whether the goals and objectives of the organization have been achieved. Alternatively, town hall meetings could be an opportunity where employees share their views freely by interacting with their managers. Most importantly, employers must have a clear idea of what they want to measure or the results that they want to assess; for good practice, they should measure what employees are doing, not only what they are thinking and feeling. Are they doing things that deliver brilliant customer service? Are they doing things that show they are working together and collaborating across the organization, sharing ideas and best practices? If that is so, the result areas to measure may include customer loyalty, employee productivity, bottom-line profit, increase in safety behavior, cost savings from employee retention, etc.

Basically, measuring engagement comes with multiple benefits to an organization, which can be summarized thus:

- It helps to identify problems as well as fix them early before they worsen.
- It helps to identify specific engagement problems in individuals, teams, departments, or even locations and to correct the underlying issues.
- Data from engagement surveys can help build a culture of trust among employees, as it shows them that their input matters.
- It strengthens the role of HR, especially in demonstrating the connection between employee engagement and business performance, which can be used to build business cases for future employee engagement initiatives.

Metrics in Measuring Employee Engagement:

Generally, the global employee engagement level has fallen to 21% as of 2024. However, the level may differ from country to country or company to company, for example, in the United States, this stands at 31%, but for the best-practice organizations, it is about 70%. The implication is that in most countries and organizations, disengagement is on the rise, and the cost to the global economy is humongous; if all employees are engaged, there would be a $9.6 trillion boost in productivity (Gallup's Report, 2025). According to Gallup (2025), engaged employees outperform disengaged employees by up to 23% in terms of profitability; boost productivity up to 18%; improve retention rate by 40%, and increase customer satisfaction by 10%. On the other hand, disengagement can lead to 81% higher absenteeism rates, 64% more safety incidents, and 41% lower quality products.

It is on this background that measuring engagement has become so important to HR practitioners for two reasons: to understand that disengagement can hurt morale in organizations, turning down progress, and in most cases the disengaged employees would exit; and secondly, to understand the whole dynamics organizational process and at the same time influence key outcomes like customer satisfaction, retention rate, innovation and productivity. The following are some of the effective ways of measuring employee engagement:

Annual employee engagement surveys:

This can be used to gauge employee engagement by identifying problems and addressing them. The surveys are aimed at gathering feedback from employees and, by extension, provide invaluable insights and data to inform organizations of their engagement levels. It helps to identify trends, areas of strength, and uncover potential issues before they escalate into more significant problems. Furthermore, data collected can be used to make informed decisions and deploy strategies aimed at enhancing employee experience, such as learning programs, career development opportunities, work–life integration, recognition, and incentive programs. Asking for employee feedback through surveys goes a long way to show that their voices matter and indicates open communication and transparency, which are all vital to fostering employee engagement.

The best employee engagement surveys should be a mix of questions that cover various aspects of the employee experience, such as employee satisfaction, workplace environment, career development opportunities, leadership and management styles, company culture and values, job role, and responsibilities, etc. Some key elements that make up a good annual employee engagement survey include, but are not limited to, these:

- Clear Objectives: First, determine which aspect of engagement you want to assess, and this clarity of purpose ensures that the instrument remains focused, and the data collected is actionable.
- Concise Questions: They must be unambiguous, easy to understand, and directly relevant to what the survey is intended to examine.
- A Mixed Method of Research: consider a mixed methods approach, as this allows for a richer and more comprehensive understanding of engagement levels and the factors and their impacts.
- Instrument Validity and Reliability: Instrument reliability is the degree of consistency with which it measures the attributes it is supposed to be measuring (Creswell &Creswell, 2018). Before distributing the survey, consider the input of other HR professionals, seasoned researchers, and data analysts, or a pilot test to enhance the validity and reliability of the instrument.

The validity and reliability could be further examined using values of Cronbach's Alpha. This gives it more field validity and reliability.

- Anonymity and Confidentiality: It is important to let all employees know that their responses will not only be anonymous but also confidential. The method of confidentiality would prevent any information from being available to anyone who is not directly involved in the study. Through anonymity, participants remain unidentified throughout the study. This guarantees there won't be any invasion of privacy.
- Context and Expectation: This includes a brief introduction to the purpose of the research, the estimated time of completion, and how the results will be used. With this background set, it helps employees understand the importance of their participation and how their feedback will contribute to meaningful organizational changes.
- Internal Benchmarking: It is good to design surveys to track changes over time so that results can be compared across different periods or departments. This would mean including consistent questions that will help to identify trends, measure the impact of initiatives, and pinpoint areas where engagement is improving or declining.
- Follow-up with Action: After the analysis and findings from the survey, develop a clear action plan based on the data, communicate it to employees, and provide regular updates on its progress. There is also a need to follow up with action, as this assures employees that their input matters and reinforces the importance of future surveys.

Employee pulse surveys:

Unlike annual engagement surveys, pulse surveys are quick, focused surveys designed to capture real-time feedback from employees on specific engagement strategies, and to pinpoint areas for improvement, promote open communication, and help their companies respond more promptly to pressing issues. They are frequent surveys meant to take the "pulse "of an organization, gauge how people are feeling or thinking at a given moment. It is like the equivalent of checking your body vitals to have a first-hand grasp of what is going on. These surveys are usually shorter and easier to fill out, and employees can receive them monthly or quarterly. Employee pulse surveys have many advantages, including:

- Gathering regular feedback on how motivated and satisfied employees are at work. This singular action makes them feel valued and respected, with a strong perception that the employer cares about their welfare.
- The feedback loops help employers understand how well the initiatives deployed are doing, and how they can improve, fostering a culture of continuous growth.
- It promotes a culture of open communication where employees give honest feedback so that the organization can understand their needs and make proactive changes.
- The real-time data at the company's disposal helps them gain insight into key areas for improvement and make informed, strategic decisions that support organizational objectives.

- It can help employers quickly identify gaps, give workers resources, and improve key parameters like recognition, performance, and retention rates.

Exit and stay interviews:

Exit interviews are conducted after an employee has resigned or is about to leave an organization. It is aimed at understanding why the employee is leaving; gathering feedback on the company's culture, leadership, and processes, and identifying trends in turnover. Without fear of negative repercussions, their feedback is likely to be more honest and help you understand how organizations can improve engagement and retention. They are no longer concerned about retaliation or consequences for speaking their minds, compared to employees who intend to stay. On the other hand, stay interviews are conducted while the employees, particularly high performers and long- tenured staff, are still working with the organization. The purpose is to discover what keeps them engaged, what would make their experience better, and to identify potential retention risks. Stay interviews are proactive and preventive, while exit interviews are like post-mortems.

One-on-one and small group meetings:

While surveys are popular ways of measuring employee engagement, there is a great need for direct human interaction. Hence, the use of one-on-one or group meetings. This is a human-centered way to measure engagement, providing intimate conversations into employees' experience that no spreadsheet can replicate. Check-ins by managers or regular one-on-one meetings between managers and their reports are a good way to measure employee satisfaction or other outcomes that may impact engagement. Additionally, some managers may organize small group sessions or focus groups where they meet employees to drill down into issues uncovered by engagement surveys. These involve managers leading guided discussions on topics and inviting employees to share their thoughts. Both one-on-one meetings and small group meetings are better ways of obtaining qualitative data when compared to surveys that are impersonal. The leader can detect disengagement not just from what the employee said, but how it was said, via the tone, body language, and even silence speaks volumes. It is advisable that this approach should not be used as a standalone, but in conjunction with other strategies for effectiveness in the measurement process. Some of the things to look for during group or one-on-one meetings are:

- The level of passion with which they speak about their job, the energy, and the enthusiasm.
- The extent to which they understand their roles and responsibilities, and how they contribute to the overall objectives.
- If the employees are seeking to learn and grow, and if there are opportunities for that
- How much do they feel encouraged and supported by their supervisors, etc.

Employee net promoter score (ENPS) surveys:

These are modern tools for measuring employee loyalty. This is based on a single-question survey, in which employees are asked how likely they are to recommend their organization as a place to work. The question may be framed this way: On a scale of 0 to 10, how likely are you to recommend this company as a great place to work? The responses can be categorized thus:

- Promoters (9-10) - represent highly satisfied and loyal employees.
- Passives (7-8) – represent employees who are content but not enthusiastic.
- Detractors (0-6) represent unhappy employees and potentially disengaged.

The survey is given out regularly, and the responses are used to measure employee sentiments, including changes over time. This has become important given the fast-changing workplace, whereby organizations are increasingly seeking agile, data-driven methods to understand how their employees feel about their work environment. As a reflection of how employees perceive their workplace, a high eNPS would mean a healthy culture, strong leadership, and meaningful work, whereas a low score, on the other hand, could be an indication of underlying issues such as poor communication, lack of recognition, or burnout. Organizations with high eNPS are likely to benefit from lower turnover rates, higher productivity, stronger employer branding, and teamwork. This is because it fosters a sense of loyalty and ownership among employees and can unlock deep insight into the health of the organization.

Turnover, productivity, and absenteeism tracking: When measuring engagement, it is vital to keep an eye on indirect indicators that could reveal employee engagement problems. One of the metrics that provides insights into employee engagement is the rate of turnover. Employee turnover refers to the rate at which employees leave an organization either voluntarily or involuntarily. High turnover often is an indication of disengagement, dissatisfaction, or misalignment with company culture, while a low turnover rate, especially among high performers, suggests a strong engaging workplace culture.

Another metric to look out for is the rate of absenteeism. Absenteeism refers to frequent or unexplained absences from work. While occasional absences are normal, chronic absenteeism can be a red flag and an indication deeper issue related to employee engagement. Tracking the average number of absences compared to the total number of possible workdays in each period is another indirect way of measuring employee engagement. When high-flyers leave the company for other companies, it may reflect a lack of growth, recognition, or purpose within the organization. Additionally, benchmarking turnover rates against industry standards can reveal whether an organization is retaining talent effectively. Therefore, low-rate absenteeism typically correlates with high engagement, where people feel valued and connected to their work; more likely to show up consistently and contribute fully.

Lastly, productivity measures how efficiently an employee completes his/her tasks and contributes to organizational goals. Engaged employees are more likely to be fully committed to their roles and work to their full potential. By implication, keeping track of various productivity metrics can help organizations spot engagement issues. Some of the sub-metrics or indirect metrics to watch include- revenue per employee, project completion rate, sales growth, employee utilization, total cost of workforce, etc. Engaged employees tend to be more focused, proactive, and innovative, and are also likely to put more effort into their work, which could boost productivity. On the other hand, productivity often drops when employees are disengaged.

Measuring turnover, productivity, and absenteeism is more than operational metrics; they are behavioral mirrors reflecting the emotional and psychological state of a workforce. When these factors are monitored closely, organizations can proactively address disengagement, foster a culture of support, and build a workplace where employees thrive.

Employee Satisfaction Index:

This evaluates how well a workplace meets employees' expectations in areas like job responsibilities, leadership support, and workplace conditions. Regular surveys help gather feedback on various aspects of the work environment, including job satisfaction, management effectiveness, and team dynamics. The surveys are aimed at deriving responses from questions like this:

- How satisfied are you with your present job?
- To what extent does your job meet your expectations?
- How close is your current job to your ideal job?
- The response to the above questions is scored ranging from 0 to 100, with higher scores reflecting greater satisfaction and engagement, while lower scores may indicate a disengaged workforce.

The Downside of Employee Engagement:

The opposite of engagement is disengagement. Disengagement can be defined as the decoupling of the psychological self from the work role and involves people retracting and guarding themselves during role performances. Also, they may be in the habit of floating and simply occupying spaces, spending time, and not putting energy or passion into their work. Disengagement not only affects the individual who is disengaged but also the rest of the organization's success, because they are disconnected physically and emotionally. In every organization, there are some employees who would remain disengaged and would not respond despite organizational efforts to motivate them. One thing is sure- disengaged employees have uncoupled themselves emotionally and cognitively from the work situation. They have the tendency to display near-zero commitment to their jobs, incomplete role performance, lack of autonomy, or feelings that the job has little meaning (O'Donnell, 2025)

Despite the success stories of employee engagement, many companies are witnessing a troubling decline in engagement levels. The erosion of enthusiasm and connection to work is due to multifaceted and interwoven factors, among which are rapid organizational changes, hybrid and remote work complexities, outdated performance management systems, and shifting customer and employee expectations. In today's fast-changing workplace, a lot of things are happening at the same time, such as organizational change, mergers and acquisitions, and digital transformation, which can destabilize employees since they are evolving too fast and in greater dimensions. A situation where changes occur too frequently and without clear communication would leave employees in a state of uncertainty and multiply their anxiety, thereby causing them to feel insecure about their jobs. This is more disturbing when organizational values, teams, or workflows shift rapidly; employees may struggle to find meaning or connection in their work. Such an atmosphere can erode trust and disengage even the most resilient employees. Inasmuch as organizational change is good, it must be planned and implemented in phases and allow for employees' buy-in. In addition, the rise of hybrid and remote work also comes with flexibility and autonomy, which, on one hand, encourages engagement. But on the other hand, it causes isolation and disconnection as employees are excluded from team dynamics, resulting in loss of belonging. Remote work can lack nuance, making it harder to build relationships or resolve conflicts, or create disparities in visibility, access to leadership, and career advancement.

High employee engagement, if not properly managed, can lead to burnout, negatively impacting employee well-being, performance, and productivity. Excessive work demands and pressure can pave the way for exhaustion and fatigue, and by extension, impact an individual's physical and emotional health. Burnout is defined as a psychological syndrome characterized by exhaustion, cynicism, and inefficacy, which is experienced in response to chronic job stressors. Therefore, the warning signs of burnout include exhaustion, decreased motivation, and increased cynicism, and they become evident when the drivers of engagement become weak or misguided due to improper plans and implementations. According to Maslach et al (2004), there were six areas of work-life that could lead to either burnout or engagement, and they are: workload, control, rewards and recognition, community and social support, perceived fairness, and values. The authors argue that job engagement is associated with a sustainable workload, feelings of choice and control, appropriate recognition and reward, a supportive work community, fairness and justice, and meaningful and valued work.

Unfortunately, the rise of remote work and digital connectivity has blurred the boundaries between personal and professional life, and many employees are subjected to constant pressure, shifting employee expectations, and working for long periods of time without breaks or foregoing their lunch to accomplish assigned projects within a given deadline. The most challenging aspect is that in today's workplace, you find employees and customers who are aware of rights and have expectations, ranging from transparency to purpose-driven missions and ethical leadership. For example, employees are seeking alignment between their personal values and organizational purpose. Yet the younger generation of workers is craving work-life integration, mental health, autonomy, and empowerment-areas where many companies lag. Also, there is no doubt that employees who feel disconnected from their companies and their brand promises may struggle to deliver genuine service. Therefore, when any organization fails to meet these expectations substantially, it may be out of touch with what matters, and the employees may slide into disengagement.

- To mitigate these risks, organizations should place emphasis on work-life balance and implement initiatives that promote employee well-being. It is highly important to provide resources and support, encourage open communication, and recognize employee efforts while addressing the negative consequences of high employee engagement. It is imperative for business practitioners to prevent mounting disengagement and burnout rates in employees and implement effective engagement-building techniques to accrue a competitive advantage. It also becomes essential for managers to determine the causes of disengagement and plug the gaps with a view to strengthening engagement areas (Ahlowalia et al, 2004: 314). While engaged employees are more likely to actively contribute to improving business processes and the bottom line, disengaged employees take less initiative, limiting opportunities for creativity and long-term business development. There are some of the early warning signs of disengagement to watch out for, and when identified, take proactive steps to re-engage employees to avert a full-blown disengagement. A few of the signs are as follows:

- Poor leadership and communication: inconsistent communication, lack of transparency, and micromanagement of employees can erode trust and lower morale. Disengaged employees tend to withdraw from conversations, contribute fewer ideas, and avoid collaboration.
- Low morale: Employees may lose motivation, enthusiasm, and passion for their work and become frustrated, indifferent, and detached.
- Performance metrics: When employees feel that performance management systems have become punitive, rigid, or irrelevant, they may become disengaged.

- Frequent absenteeism: Watch it when many employees start calling in sick, arriving late to work, or taking extended breaks.
- Aging workforce: Engagement levels decline as length of service increases.
- Increase level of turnover: While some levels of turnover are normal, a noticeable increase suggests deeper engagement issues.
- Declining productivity: Missed deadlines, decreasing work quality, and lack of attention to detail are all signs that someone is no longer fully invested.
- Negative work environment: A toxic or stressful workplace, job insecurity, workplace harassment, lack of psychological safety, conflict between team members, and lack of respect for human dignity all have a big negative impact on engagement.
- Feeling unheard and unrecognized: When employees start feeling that their work goes unnoticed or that their opinions are not valued, or their hard work is not appreciated can lead to disengagement.
- Stagnant growth: lack of career progression, skill development, or new challenges can make even the most loyal team members lose interest.

References

Abdou, A. (2024). 13 Benefits of employee engagement, and why it's so important.

https://www.applauz.me/resources/benefits-of-employee-engagement

Anitha, J. (2014). Determinants of employee engagement and their impact on employee performance.

International Journal of Productivity and Performance Management, 63(3), 308–323. https://doi.org/10.1108/IJPPM-01-2013-0008

Bhavani, S. A., Sharavan, S., & Arpitha, S. (2015). A study effectiveness of employee engagement in automobile industry.

International Journal of Economics & Management Sciences, 4(10), 5. https://doi.org/10.4172/2162-6359.1000295

Balakrishnan, C., & Masthan, D. (2013). Impact of internal communication on employee engagement. A study at Delhi International Airport.

International Journal of Scientific and Research Publications, 3(8), 1–13. http://www.ijsrp.org/research-paper-0813/ijsrp-p2059.pdf

Bui, D. H., & Le, A. T. T. (2023). Improving employee engagement through organizational culture in the travel industry: Perspective from a developing country during Covid-19 pandemic.

Cogent Business & Management, 10(2).

https://doi.org/10.1080/23311975.2023.2232589

Cook, J. & Wall, T. (1980). New work attitude measures of trust, organizational commitment, and personal need non-fulfillment.

Journal of Occupational Psychology, 53(1), 39-52. https://doi.org/10.1111/j.2044-8325.1980.tb00005.

DecisionWise (2025). Seven ways of defining employee engagement.

https://decisionwise.com/resources/articles/defining-employee-engagement/

Dromey, J. (2014). Employee engagement: The evidence. CIPD.

https://www.cipd.org/uk/knowledge/reports/employee-engagement-evidence/

Engage for Success. (2014). The evidence: Employee engagement task force–One year on. https://www.engageforsuccess.org/wpcontent/uploads/2014/04/The-Evidence.pdf

Frei, R., & Morris, D. (2019). 2019 employee engagement & modern workplace report. Bonusly. https://cdn2.hubspot.net/hubfs/1973303/2019-employee-engagement-and-modern-workplace-report-1.pdf

Forker, E. (2025). Employee recognition that works. https://business.wisc.edu/news/recognition-that-works-assistant-professor-ewelina-forker-shares-strategies-that-boost-engagement-and-retention/

Gallup (2023).

https://www.gallup.com/cliftonstrengths/en/357065/how-successful-people-lead-skills.aspx

Gallup (2025). Employee engagement.

https://www.gallup.com/394373/indicator-employee-engagement.aspx

Hackman, J. R., & Oldham, G. R. (1980). Work redesign. Addison-Wesley.

Harter, J. K., Schmidt, F. L., Agrawal, S., & Plowman, S. K. (2013). The relationship between engagement at work and organizational outcomes: 2012 Q12® meta-analysis. Gallup, Inc.

https://employeeengagement.com/wp-content/uploads/2013/04/2012-Q12-Meta-Analysis-Research-Paper.pdf

Judeh, M. (2021). Effect of work environment on employee engagement: mediating role of ethical decision-making. Problems and Perspectives in Management. 19(3), 220-229.

Kahn, W. A. (1990). Psychological conditions of personal engagement and disengagement at work. Academy of Management Journal, 33(4), 692–724.

https://doi.org/10.5465/256287

Karunamurthy, A. (2024). The role of organizational culture in driving employee engagement: Insights and implications.

Quing International Journal of Multidisciplinary Scientific Research and Development. 3(3):26-32. DOI: 10.54368/qijmsrd.3.3.0009.

Kazimoto, P. (2016). Employee engagement and organizational performance of retails enterprises.

American Journal of Industrial and Business Management, 6(4), 516–525.

https://doi.org/10.4236/ajibm.2016.64047

Kristof-Brown, A. L., Zimmerman, R. D., & Johnson, E. C. (2005). Consequences of individuals' fit at work: A meta-analysis of person–job, person–organization, person–group, and person–supervisor fit. Personnel Psychology, 58(2), 281–342.

Kumar, N. (2024). How to improve engagement with learning and development.

https://elearningindustry.com/how-to-improve-employee-engagement-with-learning-and-development

Kumar, J., Prasad, V. B., Mohideen, U. K. S., Singh, S., Chinthamu, N., & Jaiswal, R. (2024). Employee engagement and retention: Strategies for success. Journal of Informatics Education and Research, 4(2), 1–15.

https://doi.org/10.52783/jier.v4i2.1263

Macey et al (2009). Employee engagement: Tools for analysis, practice, and competitive advantage. USA: Wiley-Blackwell & Sons Limited.

MacLeod, D., & Clarke, N. (2012). Engaging for success: Enhancing performance through employee engagement. UK Government.

https://assets.publishing.service.gov.uk/government/uploads/system/uploads/attachment_data/file/215458/david-macleod-report.pdf

Malik, A. (2028). Strategic performance and commitment management. In Strategic Human Resource Management and Employee Relations (pp.85-91). Springer.

Martin, J., A., & others. (2014). Determinants of employee engagement and their impact on employee performance.

International Journal of Productivity and Performance Management, 63(3), 308–323. https://doi.org/10.1108/IJPPM-01-2013-0008

O'Donnell, R. (2025). 8 Costly drawbacks of high employee engagement you must know.

https://social-hire.com/blog/small-business/8-costly-drawbacks-of-high-employee-engagement-you-must-know

Pauline, L., Nicole, G., Leon, M., & Alexander, W. (2010).

Leadership and trust: Their effect on knowledge sharing and team performance. Management Learning, 41(4), 473-491.

https://doi.org/10.1177/1350507610362036

Phifer, L. (2023). The 2023 word of the year: "Employee engagement".

https://www.why-work.org/blog/the-2023-word-of-the-year-employeeengagement?utm_source=chatgpt.com

Phillip, J., & Juster, R. (2014). Determinants of employee engagement and their impact on employee performance.

International Journal of Productivity and Performance Management, 63(3), 308–323. https://doi.org/10.1108/IJPPM-01-2013-0008

Rafferty, A. E., & Griffin, M. A. (2005). Dimension of transformational leadership: Conceptual and empirical extensions. The Leadership Quarterly, 16(3), 329–354.

https://doi.org/10.1016/j.leaqua.2005.03.009

Ravi, D. (2023). An impact of organizational culture on employee engagement in corporate sector.

https://www.researchgate.net/publication/375860250_ ANIMPACT_OF_ORGANIZATIONAL_CULTURE_ ON_EMPLOYEE_EN GAGEMENT_IN_CORPORATE_SECTOR

Rosso, B. D., Dekas, K. H., & Wrzesniewski, A. (2010). On the meaning of work: Theoretical integration and

review. Research in Organizational Behavior, 30,
91–127.

Russell, K. (2013, May 2). Making employee engagement
engaging. HRZone.

https://hrzone.com/making-employee-engagement-engaging/

Saks, A. M. (2006). Antecedents and consequences of
employee engagement.

Journal of Managerial Psychology, 21(7), 600–619.
https://doi.org/10.1108/02683940610690169

Samtharam, S. R., & Baskaran, S. (2023). Work-life
integration and workplace flexibility on life
satisfaction, work productivity, and
organizational commitment: Contextual study.

International Journal of Academic Research in Business
and Social Sciences, 13(2), 1276–1289.

Schein, E. H. (2010). Organizational culture and leadership (4th ed).

Jossey-Bass Scholz, C. (1987). Corporate culture and strategy: The problem of strategic fit. Long Range Planning, 20(4), 78–87.

Shantz, A., Alfes, K., & Truss, C. (2013). The role of employee engagement in the relationship between job design and task performance, citizenship and deviant behaviors.

The International Journal of Human Resource Management, 24(13), 2608–2627. https://doi.org/10.1080/09585192.2012.744334

SHRM (2024). Employee recognition can go a long way, but it has to be done right. https://www.shrm.org/topics-tools/flagships/all-things-work/employee-recognition-can-go-long-way-but-has-to-be-done-right

Sundaray, B. K. (2011). Employee engagement: A driver of organizational effectiveness.

European Journal of Business and Management, 3(8), 53–60. https://www.iiste.org/Journals/index.php/EJBM/article/view/600/490

TeamOut (2025). 30 Employee engagement statistics that will transform-your team building strategy in 2025.

https://www.teamout.com/blog-post/employee-engagement-statistics

Towers Perrin. (2003). working today: Understanding what drives employee engagement.

https://studylib.net/doc/12886509/understanding-
what-drives-employee-engagement-working-
tod..

Torrington, D., Hall, L., Taylor, S., & Atkinson, C. (2011).
Human Resource Management (8th Ed.). Pearson
Education.

Truss et al. (2014). Job Design and Employee
Engagement.

https://www.engageforsuccess.org/wp-
content/uploads/2021/01/Job-Design-and-
Employee-Engagement-Katie-Truss-et-al-
11.pdf

Vintage Circle (2025). Unlocking the 23 Benefits of
Employee Engagement in the Workplace.

https://www.vantagecircle.com/en/blog/benefits-of-
employee-engagement/

Wooll, M. (2022). Work-life integration: What it is and

5 ways to develop it.

https://www.betterup.com/blog/work-life-integration